Newsrooms and the Disruption of the Internet

Newsrooms and the Disruption of the Internet is an insightful account of what happened when the internet first arrived in the 1990s and early 2000s in the recently computerized, but still largely unchanged, newspaper industry.

Providing a focused narrative of how the internet disrupted news collection, editing, presentation and dissemination, the book examines the role of the internet from helpful adjunct to extension to, eventually, successor to the traditional print product. Experiments by large national newspaper "brands" and other first-adopters in the 1990s are described, tracing the slow adoption of the internet by chains and large metro papers, followed by smaller daily and weekly newspapers by the early 2000s. The book describes the changes that arrived as more "Web 2.0" technologies become prevalent and as social media shifted the news-media landscape in the mid-to-late 2000s, ultimately changing how most people in the West consumed and thought of "the news."

This book is intended for academics and researchers in the fields of journalism studies, history of technology, and media studies, especially those interested in transitions from analog to digital technology, and the initial adoption of the commercial internet.

Will Mari is Assistant Professor at the Manship School of Mass Communication, Louisiana State University, USA. He is a media historian and interested in analog-to-digital transitions in journalism and the history of media technology, more broadly. He received his PhD from the University of Washington, USA, and his MPhil from Wolfson College, Cambridge, UK.

Disruptions: Studies in Digital Journalism
Series editor: Bob Franklin

Disruptions refers to the radical changes provoked by the affordances of digital technologies that occur at a pace and on a scale that disrupts settled understandings and traditional ways of creating value, interacting and communicating both socially and professionally. The consequences for digital journalism involve far reaching changes to business models, professional practices, roles, ethics, products and even challenges to the accepted definitions and understandings of journalism. For Digital Journalism Studies, the field of academic inquiry which explores and examines digital journalism, disruption results in paradigmatic and tectonic shifts in scholarly concerns. It prompts reconsideration of research methods, theoretical analyses and responses (oppositional and consensual) to such changes, which have been described as being akin to 'a moment of mind-blowing uncertainty'.

Routledge's book series, ***Disruptions: Studies in Digital Journalism***, seeks to capture, examine and analyse these moments of exciting and explosive professional and scholarly innovation which characterize developments in the day-to-day practice of journalism in an age of digital media, and which are articulated in the newly emerging academic discipline of Digital Journalism Studies.

Newsrooms and the Disruption of the Internet
A Short History of Disruptive Technologies, 1990–2010
Will Mari

News Agencies
Anachronism or Lifeblood of the Media System?
Stephen Jukes

For more information about this series, please visit: www.routledge.com/Disruptions/book-series/DISRUPTDIGJOUR

Newsrooms and the Disruption of the Internet

A Short History of Disruptive Technologies, 1990–2010

Will Mari

Routledge
Taylor & Francis Group
LONDON AND NEW YORK

First published 2022
by Routledge
4 Park Square, Milton Park, Abingdon, Oxon OX14 4RN

and by Routledge
605 Third Avenue, New York, NY 10158

Routledge is an imprint of the Taylor & Francis Group, an informa business

British Library Cataloguing-in-Publication Data
A catalogue record for this book is available from the British Library

Library of Congress Cataloging-in-Publication Data
Names: Mari, Will (William), author.
Title: Newsrooms and the disruption of the internet : a short history of disruptive technologies, 1990–2010 / Will Mari.
Description: London ; New York : Routledge, 2022. | Series: Disruptions | Includes bibliographical references and index.
Identifiers: LCCN 2021052989 (print) | LCCN 2021052990 (ebook) | ISBN 9780367342975 (hardback) | ISBN 9781032249636 (paperback) | ISBN 9780429324871 (ebook)
Subjects: LCSH: Journalism—United States—History—20th century. | Journalism—United States—History—21st century. | Online journalism—United States—History—21st century. | Journalism—Technological innovations—United States.
Classification: LCC PN4867.2 .M335 2022 (print) | LCC PN4867.2 (ebook) | DDC 071/.309049—dc23/eng/20211201
LC record available at https://lccn.loc.gov/2021052989
LC ebook record available at https://lccn.loc.gov/2021052990

ISBN: 978-0-367-34297-5 (hbk)
ISBN: 978-1-032-24963-6 (pbk)
ISBN: 978-0-429-32487-1 (ebk)

DOI: 10.4324/9780429324871

Typeset in Times New Roman
by Apex CoVantage, LLC

Contents

Acknowledgments

Whenever an author is fortunate enough to write a sequel in a book series, it is probably good to begin with a sincere thank-you to one's editor, in this case Bob Franklin. Bob shepherded my first book, *A Short History of Disruptive Journalism Technologies*, from imagination to completion, and had faith enough in me to give me another go at it, this time moving from a short history of newsroom computerization to that of newsroom internetization. He provided me with encouragement and practical advice, connections and courage. He remains the best of editors, in that regard—that kind that not only wants to give you a shot but also makes you better.

This book could not have been completed without a great deal of help from a number of other people, as well.

I should thank the students, staff and my fellow faculty at the Manship School of Mass Communication at LSU. Specifically, I am grateful to Manship for providing the intellectual space and research funding, via the Bill and Avis Ross family's generous support, to complete much-needed thinking, research and travel for this project. Our late dean, Martin Johnson, was immensely supportive of the book, as has been our interim dean, Josh Grimm. Thank you, both—Martin for believing in me enough to hire me, and Josh for honoring Martin's legacy so well. My colleagues at Manship, including Sheryl Kennedy Haydel and David Stamps, now at Loyola University in New Orleans and Bentley University in Boston, respectively, have also been kind, cheering me on while I was fairly new to them as their friend. Our former dean, Jerry Ceppos, was especially generous in letting himself be subjected to interviews, questions, emails, Twitter DMs and various requests for help—Jerry is a class act and a genuine mensch.

Any good media-history project's acknowledgments would not be complete without an earnest thank-you to LSU Libraries' hard-working librarians and archivists. Of special note, Ms. Rebecca Kelley, our library liaison to Manship, and Mr. Jacob Fontenot, our head of interlibrary loan, were extremely helpful and creative in assisting me in this project, preserving the important physical, bound volumes of trade publications, requesting books and articles on my behalf, and generally making sure I had everything I needed to complete this project, despite the ongoing 2020–2021 pandemic.

My undergraduate research assistant, Ms. Salena Ali, also a McNair Scholar, spent a great deal of her valuable time hunting down volumes of *American Journalism Review*, taking notes on them, and finding other material, transcribing it, and basically being awesome with all her research help.

I had the opportunity to travel briefly to the Media Archeology Lab at the University of Colorado at Boulder, as part of the research for this project, and that visit was instrumental in shaping my thinking. I need to go back! Thank you, Dr. Lori Emerson, the lab's founding director, and Dr. Libi Rose Striegl, the lab's manager, for graciously granting me access and taking the time to talk through my somewhat half-baked ideas. Josh Shepperd, also at UC-Boulder, has similarly served as an inspiration and sounding board on my project.

Merci beaucoup [thank you very much] to my colleagues at the Université de Montréal, namely, the profoundly inspiring Paperology Reading and Activity Group (PAPG), part of the Artefact Lab in the Department of Communication, especially Juliette De Maeyer, Ghislain Thibault, Aleksandra Kaminska and Alysse Kushinski—you have helped me make connections in the long analog-to-digital transition that journalism is (still) undergoing.

To my dear friends in my writing group, the Notion Club, back in my adopted hometown of Seattle, in Washington state, especially Elise Stephens, Carrie Kahler, Nick Escobar, Julie Zehnder, Chris and Natasha Lim—as well as those now spread out across the country, including Scott and Hannah Wilder, Casey Karbowski and Kevin Mosher, among others—thank you for your enduring friendship during this long pandemic. Other Seattle colleagues and friends, including Bethany and David Slater, Matt Bellinger and Clint Bryan, need a shout-out here too.

My AEJMC History Division colleagues, including Teri Finneman, Cayce Myers and Maddie Liseblad, have been supportive of me throughout this process. I appreciate you!

My former dissertation adviser, Richard Kielbowicz, provided me with copies of books and trade publications *again*, often through physical mail, at his own expense, that I used as part of my project—thank you, sir. This is the third book that you have helped make far better.

And while it may seem a *tad* silly, I need to thank my plucky and cheerful choodle, Roux, for forcing me to take writing and thinking breaks.

Lastly, I need to thank my wife and fellow scholar, Dr. Ruth Moon Mari, for her help and ideas. It is to you, and to our future baby boy, that this book is dedicated. I love you both like crazy.

1 Introduction

Newsrooms and the disruption of the internet

The newspaper industry was nearly destroyed, and may yet be killed off entirely, by the internet. Or so the story goes. That is not entirely true, but remains a common account of the short history of the internet and the news.

When thinking about recent events, it can be tempting to seek out simplicity—good versus bad choices about competing business strategies, a particular technology's adoption or lack of it, or a media company's shares in a technology start-up, but the reality was and remains messy. Looking back from the early 2020s, our hindsight offers clarity, but it is important to remember that for those who came before us, foresight was as fuzzy for them as it is for us.

This short book is a history of how the journalism industry in North America, and to some degree in the United Kingdom, grappled with what to do with the rise of the civilian internet. It is not comprehensive. While it does contain some oral history, others have done a great deal more in that arena, and more work remains to be completed, especially as the first generation of online news workers grows older.[1] The narrative takes off where my previous book left off, namely, with the computerization of US, Canadian and British newsrooms by the early 1990s.[2]

The internet brought with it a host of changes, of course, but not all of them were immediately apparent. The browsers used to navigate the "World Wide Web" were not necessarily easy or intuitive to navigate. With dial-up speeds, videos were either impossible to upload and play or, if they were present, short and of low resolution, choppy and prone to freezing up. Audio content was little better, though that had more early success. Even photos and gifs were relatively rare—scrolling walls of text were most common. For many savvy prognosticators, the future still seemed, at least for the foreseeable future, to belong to print media and over-the-air and cable broadcasters. Yes, the internet would probably eventually get faster and flashier, and might even contain such wonders as immersive virtual reality

DOI: 10.4324/9780429324871-1

(though it seems we are still working on that prediction), but not for another generation.

In this, these forecasters were not incorrect. That is why giving out content for free seemed to make sense, at least initially—it was only later relabeled as the so-called "original sin" of the internet.[3] The emergence of online journalism (often described with the original mechanical spelling, as "on-line") was, in terms of technological timescales, swift, of course, faster than the previous adoption of mainframes, minicomputers with terminals, then personal computers, for the generation of journalists who had worked in the latter decades of the Cold War. They had seen change. But their older selves and their successors would of course see far more, and far more quickly.

But is important to remember—and this is a point I will return to throughout this study and attempt to nuance—that the newspaper industry, along with such sectors as finance and the academy, was in fact a successful early adopter of the internet, at least in terms of establishing a recognizable online presence and pioneering the partnership of the analog and the digital. Many editors and publishers were savvy in that adoption in ways that deserve elaboration beyond the simple dismissal of publishers as "slow to react," or "behind" in their incorporation of digital tools. In fact, some of the first places to gather on both the proto-internet of the 1980s and then the initial "web-"based internet of the early 1990s were, in fact, via newspaper sites and their message boards, forums and early comment threads.

What first was heralded as a helpful adjunct, then as an extension, and then, eventually, a successor to the traditional print product, internet-based news, would quickly become helpful and then unavoidable. Beginning with experiments by large national newspaper "brands" in the early 1990s and other first-adopters, leading to the slow but steady adoption by chains and large metro papers by the late 1990s, and then by smaller daily and weekly newspapers by the early to mid-2000s, the story of the internet-as-platform and then as news vehicle was neither foreordained nor necessarily one of gloom.

In fact, an infectious optimism pervaded the field. That, of course, would change as more "Web 2.0" technologies become prevalent and as social media shifted the news-media landscape from about 2000 through 2010. Yahoo and then Google News (which still relies entirely on information produced by news organizations), but also YouTube, Apple, Facebook and Twitter, among others, would change how most people in the West consumed and thought of "the news." But the nitty-gritty of that shift deserves a more complex telling.

The early internet's initial impact on the newspaper industry in context

The case of Knight Ridder shows some of the problems of future casting. One of the largest and most profitable newspaper chains in the US in the 1990s, Knight Ridder led the way in innovating online news coverage, especially in its flagship publication on the West Coast, *The San Jose Mercury News* and its Mercury Center.[4] While more about the latter's influence will be discussed later in this book, it is notable that even this company—itself no stranger to large-scale technology experiences, having sunk more than $50 million into its Viewtron experiment in the 1980s—was unable to quite predict just how much online ads would erode its substantial profitability.[5]

Planning documents from an internal 1992 report, which tried to look ahead to 2012, imagined a range of fates for the company and the newspaper industry as a whole, from a still-robust place of dominance (with an estimated, continuing set of 20-percent profit margins for many of its newspapers) to mere survival.[6] The rise of online ads was, in fact, taken into account: Craigslist's arrival was not entirely a surprise. But what these documents could not forecast was the demise of Knight Ridder itself, bought by another, large American chain, McClatchy, for $4.5 billion, in 2006 (even at that point Knight Ridder had 32 papers, many still financially stable).[7]

Craigslist and companies like it were able to move faster than expected by larger, more slow-moving (and cautious) media companies, though even this part of the story has a number of caveats. It is true to say that a new generation of online firms would go on to grab most of the lucrative share of money that came from classified ads online at this point in time, some 37 percent of the total ad revenue for North American newspapers in 1997.[8] By some estimates that was worth as much as $17 billion in that year alone (not adjusted for inflation).[9] But beyond the blow to ad revenues—arguably a near-fatal, if gradual one—the disorientation caused by the rise of online competitors was not unforeseen. Numerous accounts in the trade publications of that era, as well as in the recollections and memoirs of industry leaders, show that throughout the late 1990s and into the early 2000s there was a dawning and very real consensus that unless the field rapidly found ways to protect its ad franchise, as well as garner new readers, it faced the real possibility of extinction.

It is also unfair to pile all the blame onto Craig Newmark, the founder of Craigslist. In fact, in recent years, there has been some helpful revisionism regarding the supposedly singular role his company played in eroding online ad revenues.[10] Other recent accounts have also complicated the narrative, looking at how many, smaller, iterative decisions, instead of just a few large ones, added up to mean that by the end of the 2000s, with the start of the Great Recession, the industry was in a real, and not just anticipated or perceived crisis.[11] This more complex analysis of the impact of the internet on newspapers in particular is still drowned out by more simplistic tales. And even the more sophisticated, journalistic takes tend to focus on the future and present, and less so on the past, with some exceptions.

With all this, it is important to understand a few things about the internet of the c. 1990s and how it differs from that of today. For one thing, the internet was much smaller then, in the form of its audience and content.[12] Only a small fraction of adults were online for a number of years, and many of them were programmers or computer hobbyists. These were mostly white, relatively well-off, young to middle-aged men who had access to the internet at home due to their occupations or because they had the free time and capacity to learn how to find early web pages (and in many cases, build them). Beginning in and around 1996 and 1997, that would begin to change, as more women and older people, members of minority groups and younger users would start to log on.

But one report in 1995, for example, noted that just "5.1 percent of the nation's households . . . [were] online," with an accompanying warning "against overestimating future growth," although it was also observed that that growth could increase.[13] In 1996, the Newspaper Association of America reported that 175 dailies were available online, with 775 worldwide, with about 3.6 percent of the total population able to read them, including 1.1 million under 18.[14] While I will explore the growth of online news sites more in the next chapter, to put those population figures in perspective, 263 million people lived in the US in 1995. So that means that just shy of 9.5 million had regular access to the internet within about two years into its life as a commercial enterprise.[15] That was not an insubstantial number, but still constituted only a small fraction of the audience for more traditional media forms. It is not surprising, then, that at first many industry leaders either did not necessarily worry about getting their print readers online or at least felt they had some runway.

A present-day metaphor is a bit hard to find, but for those of us living in 2021, perhaps space tourism or fully immersive, virtual-reality platforms are a kind of rough equivalent: probably coming, but not really quite yet for most people, in most places. But that might change. And then what will people think of us? Were we "caught off guard" or "slow-footed" or just, humanly, could not predict the future, *Black Mirror* episodes aside?

The discourse of "what if" and "what next" pervades any recent history of technology, especially the internet. And with journalism, regardless of the era and platform (digital, analog or otherwise), the discourse of anxiety/skepticism/hope/potential about technology runs so deep within that industry/practice/tradition/institution as to be part of its identity. This book tries to provide a through line for scholars working on this topic in the future, a point of reference written not long after the changes (started) to settle down, and with an eye toward creating a useable narrative that other, later researchers can start from, to dig deeper into whatever aspect of early internet history and journalism they want to explore. In other words, its contribution will hopefully be one of a framework for others to follow.

Generally, the short histories that do exist on the development of the internet's impact on the newspaper industry fall into one of several categories, including:

1) despair ("the internet *has* killed journalism"); these are often written by former journalists, though the irony is that they are of course successful[16]
2) hope, or some variation on it ("the internet was not the worst thing, actually, for journalism")[17]
3) it's-still-too-soon-to-tell, or pragmatic ("here are some folks working to see if journalism will be OK with the internet")
4) scholarly ("here is one distinct part of the impact of the internet on journalism")

This study tries to take a more expansive approach, incorporating elements of the third and fourth models, and is based on primary evidence that I will outline below. It takes inspiration from Michael Shapiro, Anna Hiatt and Mike Hoyt, and their *Tales from the Great Disruption: Insights and Lessons from Journalism's Technological Transformation*, a collection of essays about journalism in the US in the late 2000s and early 2010s, with reflections going back to the 1990s.[18]

Shapiro, Hiatt and Hoyt believed that the industry was going through what they called the "Great Disruption," with some news workers believing fervently that this was a "new and exciting age," brimming with positive possibilities, and with others who worried about how journalists could sustain and support the expensive work of human-centric reporting. In both cases, the late 2000s brought an "unmooring of the basic operating tenets of the news business—simply put: that advertising, not readers, pays most of the bills."[19] But *how* that happened, and what did *not* happen, and *why*—all deserve a closer, more granular analysis, which I will attempt.

Inspirations/theory (literature review)

For a project such as this one, I am indebted to the growing body of work on internet history, including the journal *Internet Histories*, published by

Taylor & Francis and launched in 2017. Scholars such as Megan Sapnar Ankerson, Jesse Lingel, Finn Bruton, Thomas Streeter and Kevin Driscoll, among others, have imaginatively charted the history of the early internet through lenses as varied as design, business history, spam, art and message boards.[20] While these researchers do not directly address the history of journalism online, per se, their work has shaped my own understanding of the plenitude of paths-not-taken (and the contingency of those that were) during the first 10 to 20 years of the internet's existence.

Other scholars, including Joy Lisi Rankin, Mar Hicks and Charlton McIlwain, have explored the role of class, gender and race in important ways that decenter the saga of Silicon Valley when considering the history of the internet.[21] While certainly a part of the story of the computerization and then the "Internetization" of the newsroom is the parallel tale of companies such as Apple and Microsoft (which make more than extended cameos in the fate of the former), it is vital to consider the distributed nature of the origin stories (plural) of online news and of the news business' reaction to the internet.[22] Places as diverse as North Carolina and Colorado, Chicago and Los Angeles are just as critical as cities like New York and San Francisco.

Consequently, this project draws on the important theoretical interventions inherent in any focus on space and place, as well as a consideration of materiality.[23] The "things" of journalism matter, even in a digital age, lest we forget that the internet is most certainly a connected set of other technologies, whether in the form of server farms, cables, antennae, hard drives, and other hardware.[24] Thinking about how the "stuff" of early digital journalism was part of the story of the arrival of the internet helps to ground any media history in the lived experiences of news workers, which is the intention here.

Sometimes lost in the rush to describe the recent fate of journalism online are concrete case studies, but scholars, including Nikki Usher, Juliette De Maeyer, Meryl Alper and Rachel Plotnick, have shown how fully formed examples, situated in their journalistic contexts in time and space, can help to illuminate complicated moments of transition, or issues as critical to consider as gender and class.[25] Issues of power and access inform my thinking about the impact of technology on news workers, since they influence how to conceptualize issues of "adoption" and even notions such as journalistic autonomy.[26]

And reflecting the recent nature of the events that transpired to move journalism more to the internet, and not just alongside it, I incorporate the analysis of those who lived through the initial transition to the internet (though it is perhaps helpful to think of this transition as still occurring). Less than a generation ago, journalism studies' scholars and thinkers in the late 1990s and through the 2000s sought to understand what was happening to their field with the internet, and digital technology more generally, and their accounts serve as a helpful source for this study. That includes books, essays and articles by figures such as Dan Gillmor, John Pavlik, Philip Meyer, Elliot King, Patricia Dooley and Pablo Boczkowski.[27]

Boczkowski's book in particular is useful for this study, in that he was among the first to recognize that the divides between print and then-emerging digital newsrooms (in terms of labor organization, treatment of innovation, training and other factors) showcased larger challenges for the field with the move to online-first news cycles. His approach informs this project, especially when considering how newsrooms responded in complex ways to internet affordances.[28] This book draws on his and the aforementioned researchers' work for its analysis.

Methods/sources

This study relied on trade publications, including *Editor & Publisher*, the Society of Professional Journalists' *Quill*, the *American Journalism Review*, the UK-based *Press Gazette* and the *Columbia Journalism Review*. It draws from memoirs and other first-person accounts, as well as reports by corporations, including the Knight Ridder planning documents discussed earlier, and nonprofits, as well as more scholarly accounts by contemporaries living through the long analog-to-digital transition. Ample use was made of the Internet Archive's Wayback Machine to view news sites lost long ago to the ravages of rapidly moving "internet time," as David Karpf has explored.[29]

With the trade publications, the *Press Gazette* was examined from c. 2001 through c. 2008, via keyword searches on its (limited) online archive.[30] With the *Columbia Journalism Review* (*CJR*) and *Quill*, every issue from January 1992 through December 2008 was examined, with close attention paid to tables of content, photos and cutlines, and headlines that concerned the internet and journalism. Select issues of *CJR* were read through the end of 2009.

With *Editor & Publisher*, the first and third issues of the month were examined from January 1993 through December 2008, alternating with the second and fourth issues approximately every three years (the first and third issues were read for three years, and then the second and fourth for three years). Beginning with January 2000, one issue of *Editor & Publisher* was read each month, but in January 2004 and onward, the magazine moved to once-a-month publication anyway. The *American Journalism Review* was read through 2003.

The main goal of closely reading the trade publications was to create a representative sample that reflected the reality of the rank and file in the journalism industry. They were often written by upper- and middle-management figures, often directly invested in the success (or failure) of efforts to move a heavily print-focused industry online. But they also strove to take a detached tone, and especially in coverage by the *Press Gazette* and *Columbia Journalism Review*, there was often significant criticism of new-media technologies.

And by reading memoirs by newsroom leaders and innovators on both sides of the Atlantic, including by Alan Rusbridger, *The Guardian*'s editor-in-chief from 1995 into the 2010s, and Roger Fidler, who was briefly tasked with Knight Ridder's experimental project to develop news for a pre-iPad Apple tablet, this author was able to triangulate sources in helpful ways.[31]

While it is helpful to remember the power dynamics of the trade publications, care was taken to examine bottom-up, as well as top-down, perspectives. Whenever possible, the voices of women and other nonmajority individuals were highlighted, and care was also taken to examine accounts outside of Silicon Valley or New York City, following the examples discussed earlier. Furthermore, the work of Niels Brügger and Ian Milligan helped to inform this short book, with their approach to web history, which avoids tropes and instead seeks nuance and, where possible, as much information on the provenance of sites and their creators as possible.[32] Media historians Lori Emerson and David Karpf have utilized similar methods in their research and they have also influenced this project.[33]

Taken together, these sources—trade publications, contemporary material and oral-history interviews—constitute a powerful collection of evidence about an era that often falls into an analog-to-digital interregnum.[34] It can be surprisingly difficult to locate online material that is not just static from this era, and as it is still well within living memory for many of the participants, the challenges of "near history" are present, including contestation of events, and the uncertain outcomes of certain software and hardware tools. By examining several different kinds of sources, the researcher was able to identify important early trends and some paths-not-taken, which will be explored below.[35]

Overview of chapters/sections

The chapter that immediately follows this introduction overviews the first foray of newspapers into online spaces, during the mid-to-late 1990s, including such early adopters as *The New York Times*, *The Washington Post* and *The San Jose Mercury News* in the US, and *The Guardian* and the BBC in the UK. It examines discussions of these sites in the trade press, their role in the still-at-that-time print-dominated newspaper industry, and how readers responded and engaged with these sites.

The third chapter looks at large-scale responses to the internet, especially the New Century Network and its imitators, as the journalism industry briefly tried to rally around a common defense of its classified ads. How that effort gradually fell apart by early 1998 shows how hard it was to marshal a coherent approach in a field much more comfortable with acting independently, sometimes to its detriment.

The fourth chapter looks at the internet and newsgathering from the mid-1990s through the early 2000s, with a special focus on the increasing number and complexity of web-based tools, including what more affordable databases, growing reliance on email, and the early use of video and audio tools, did to the journalism industry and how some storytelling norms began to change as a result.

The fifth chapter explores the growth of the "blogosphere" and how the internet enabled more mobile journalism (the latter being the direct descendent of "portable" journalism efforts from before). It quickly digs into the arrival of amateur (i.e., "citizen") journalism and reader-sourced content, and its impact on, and its use by, journalists, as part of their newswork routines.

Finally, a concluding chapter reflects on how the internet both disrupted and did not disrupt journalism, including with the rise of paywalls, subscription services, mobile journalism and other practical tech-tool reactions to the financial rumbles of the mid-to-late 2000s in the journalism industry. As smartphones and social media further disrupted how people consumed the news, the conclusion will also point toward more recent, c. 2010 and onward research that addresses these broader issues.

Notes

1 The Shorenstein Center on Media, Politics and Public Policy's "Riptide" project is an exceptional example of this kind of effort, describing itself as an "oral history of the epic collision between journalism and digital technology from 1980 to the present," and containing dozens of interviews, with some 50 hours of video testimony. See www.digitalriptide.org/.

2 Will Mari, *A Short History of Disruptive Journalism Technologies: 1960–1990* (Abingdon, UK: Routledge, 2019).

3 This will be discussed in more detail in the second chapter; see Ethan Zuckerman, "The Internet's Original Sin It's Not Too Late to Ditch the Ad-Based Business Model and Build a Better Web," *The Atlantic*, August 14, 2014, www.theatlantic.com/technology/archive/2014/08/advertising-is-the-internets-original-sin/376041/.

4 Michael Shapiro's oral history, "The Newspaper That Almost Seized the Future," *The Columbia Journalism Review*, November–December 2011, https://archives.cjr.org/feature/the_newspaper_that_almost_seized_the_future.php.

5 David Carlson, "The History of Online Journalism," in *Digital Journalism: Emerging Media and the Changing Horizons of Journalism*, ed. Kevin Kawamoto (Lanham, MD: Rowan & Littlefield, 2003), 31–55.

6 These documents form an important part of the primary evidence used in this book, along with memoirs, trade publications, reports published by nonprofits, and correspondence with news workers from that era, among other sources that will be unpacked below.

7 David Folkenflik, "McClatchy Will Buy Knight Ridder for $4.5 Billion," *NPR*, March 13, 2006, www.npr.org/templates/story/story.php?storyId=5260417.

8 Jodi B. Cohen, "Thomson Acquires Online Classified Unit," *Editor & Publisher*, January 25, 1997, 24; Hoag Levins, "Attitude Adjustment: With Brisk Interest in Online Classified Systems Reported at Nexpo, It Appears Newspapers Are Changing Their Attitude About Internet Ads," *Editor & Publisher*, June 28, 1997, 44–45.

9 Mark Fitzgerald, "Paid Print Classifieds at Risk from Surge of Free Web Ads: Free Online Classifieds Apply Pressure to the Old Model of Advertiser-Paid Classifieds: How Do You Compete with Money-Losing Darlings of Wall Street?" *Editor & Publisher*, October 10, 1998, 8–9.

10 Alicia Shepard, "Craig Newmark and Craigslist Didn't Destroy Newspapers, They Outsmarted Them," *USA Today*, June 17, 2018, www.usatoday.com/story/opinion/2018/06/18/craig-newmark-craigslist-didnt-kill-newspapers-outsmarted-them-column/702590002/; see also Jessa Lingel, *An Internet for the People: The Politics and Promise of Craigslist* (Princeton: Princeton University Press, 2020).

11 Jack Shafer, "Don't Blame Craigslist for the Decline of Newspapers It's Fun to Beat Up on Craig Newmark for the End of Classifieds, but Papers Were Greedy, Too," *Politico*, December 13, 2016, www.politico.com/magazine/story/2016/12/craigslist-newspapers-decline-classifieds-214525/; Nicolas Lehman, "Can Journalism Be Saved? It's Going to Take a Whole New Set of Arrangements, and a New Way of Thinking, to Solve the Present Crisis," *The New York Review of Books*, February 27, 2020, www.nybooks.com/articles/2020/02/27/can-journalism-be-saved/; Jill Lepore, "Does Journalism Have a Future? In an Era of Social Media and Fake News, Journalists Who Have Survived the Print Plunge Have New Foes to Face," *The New Yorker*, January 21, 2019, www.newyorker.com/magazine/2019/01/28/does-journalism-have-a-future.

12 Lily Hay Newman, "A Trippy Visualization Charts the Internet's Growth Since 1997in2003,BarrettLyonCreatedaMapoftheInternet.In2021,HeDidItAgain—and Showed Just How Quickly It's Expanded," *Wired*, February 21, 2021, www.wired.com/story/opte-internet-map-visualization/?mbid=social_twitter&utm_brand=wired&utm_campaign=falcon&utm_medium=social&utm_socialtype=owned&utm_source=twitter/.

13 "Users of World Wide Web on the Rise," "TimesLink Adds Services," "Seattle Times Classifieds on World Wide Web," *Editor & Publisher*, August 5, 1995, 24.

14 "Chi Trib Turns Online Profit," "Number of Papers with Online Editions Tripled," "ABC, Newsweek, Washington Post Team Up Online," "Seattle Paper's Web Site Offers Classified Ads," *Editor & Publisher*, February 24, 1996, 38–43.

15 Based on data from the US Census Bureau, "Statistical Abstract of the United States: 1996, Section 1. Population," October 1996, 1, accessed

September 15, 2021, www.census.gov/library/publications/1996/compendia/statab/116ed.html.

16 For one example of this genre, see Davis Merritt, *Knight Ridder and How the Erosion of Newspaper Journalism Is Putting Democracy at Risk* (New York: American Management Association, 2005); however, I do not want to be unfair to Merritt, who has good observations and concerns from this point of time (though again ironically from a point not long before Knight Ridder found itself purchased by another corporation).

17 Some of the helpful work by Poynter or the *Columbia Journalism Review* falls within this category.

18 Michael Shapiro, Anna Hiatt and Mike Hoyt, *Tales from the Great Disruption: Insights and Lessons from Journalism's Technological Transformation* (Minneapolis, MN: Big Roundtable Books, 2015).

19 Ibid., 197–198, 203–304.

20 Megan Sapnar Ankerson, *Dot-Com Design: The Rise of a Usable, Social, Commercial Web* (New York: New York University Press, 2018); Lingel, *An Internet for the People*; Finn Brunton, *Spam: A Shadow History of the Internet* (Cambridge, MA: MIT Press, 2013); Thomas Streeter, *The Net Effect: Romanticism, Capitalism and the Internet* (New York: NYU Press, 2010); Kevin Driscoll, "Hobbyist Inter-Networking and the Popular Internet Imaginary: Forgotten Histories of Networked Personal Computing, 1978–1998" (PhD dissertation, University of Southern California, 2015).

21 Joy Lisi Rankin, *A People's History of Computing in the United States* (Cambridge, MA: Harvard University Press, 2018); Julien Mailland and Kevin Driscoll, *Minitel: Welcome to the Internet* (Cambridge, MA: MIT Press, 2017); Mar Hicks, *Programmed Inequality: How Britain Discarded Women Technologists and Lost Its Edge in Computing* (Cambridge, MA: MIT Press, 2017); Charlton McIlwain, *Black Software: The Internet and Racial Justice, from the Afronet to Black Lives Matter* (Oxford: Oxford University Press, 2019); see also Will Mari, "A Review Essay: Examining the Fraught Racial, Gendered and Class-Based Origins of the Early Internet and Its Antecedents," *Internet Histories* 4, no. 3 (2020): 349–53.

22 Constantine Passaris, "Internetization: A New Word for Our Global Economy," *The Conversation*, December 5, 2017, https://theconversation.com/internetization-a-new-word-for-our-global-economy-88013.

23 Grant Bollmer, *Materialist Media Theory: An Introduction* (New York: Bloomsbury Academic, 2019); Nikki Usher, "Newsroom Moves and the Newspaper Crisis Evaluated: Space, Place, and Cultural Meaning," *Media, Culture & Society* 37, no. 7 (2015): 1005–21; Henrik Örnebring, "Technology and Journalism-as-Labor: Historical Perspectives," *Journalism* 11, no. 57 (2010): 57–74; Juliette De Maeyer, "Digital Journalism in the Cut-and-Paste Era," *Mondes Sociaux*, April 18, 2017, accessed August 28, 2021, https://sms.hypotheses.org/9407; Rachel Moran and Nikki Usher, "Objects of Journalism, Revised: Rethinking Materiality in Journalism Studies Through Emotion, Culture and 'Unexpected Objects'," *Journalism* (December 2020).

24 Beth Whitehead, Deborah Andrews, Amip Shah and Graeme Maidment, "Assessing the Environmental Impact of Data Centres Part 1: Background, Energy Use and Metrics," *Building and Environment* 82 (August 2014): 151–59.

25 Usher, "Newsroom Moves and the Newspaper Crisis Evaluated"; De Maeyer, "Digital Journalism in the Cut-and-Paste Era"; Meryl Alper, "Portables, Luggables, and Transportables: Historicizing the Imagined Affordances of Mobile Computing," *Mobile Media & Communication* 7, no. 3 (September 2019): 322–40; Rachel Plotnick, "Tethered Women, Mobile Men: Gendered Mobilities of Typewriting," *Mobile Media & Communication* 8, no. 2 (May 2020): 188–208.
26 Henrik Örnebring, "Technology and Journalism-as-Labor: Historical Perspectives," *Journalism* 11, no. 57 (2010); see also Örnebring and Michael Karlsson's forthcoming book with the University of Missouri Press, *Journalistic Autonomy: The Genealogy of a Concept* (2022).
27 Dan Gillmor, *We the Media: Grassroots Journalism by the People, for the People* (Sebastopol, CA: O'Reilly, 2004); John Pavlik, *Journalism and New Media* (New York: Columbia University Press, 2001); Philip Meyer, *The Vanishing Newspaper: Saving Journalism in the Information Age*. 2nd ed. (Columbia, MO: University of Missouri, 2009); Elliot King, *Free for All: The Internet's Transformation of Journalism* (Evanston, IL: Northwestern University Press, 2010); Patricia L. Dooley, *The Technology of Journalism: Cultural Agents, Cultural Icons* (Evanston, IL: Northwestern University Press, 2007); Pablo Boczkowski, *Digitizing the News: Innovation in Online Newspapers* (Cambridge, MA: MIT Press, 2005).
28 Jennifer Earl and Katrina Kimport, *Digitally Enabled Social Change: Activism in the Internet Age* (Cambridge, MA: MIT Press, 2011).
29 David Karpf, "Social Science Methods in Internet Time," *Information, Communication & Society* 15, no. 5 (2012): 639–61.
30 Although the author wishes he had made more use of this source, he was able to correspond with two individuals who had close knowledge of the British journalism industry during the 1990s, and that has informed this project in helpful ways. Due to the 2020–2021 pandemic, interlibrary loan services were restricted.
31 Roger Fidler, *Touching the Future: My Odyssey from Print to Online Publishing* (Self-published, 2019); Alan Rusbridger, *Breaking News: The Remaking of Journalism and Why It Matters Now* (New York: Picador, 2017).
32 Niels Brügger, *The Archived Web: Doing History in the Digital Age* (Cambridge, MA: MIT Press, 2018); Ian Milligan, *History in the Age of Abundance? How the Web is Transforming Historical Research* (Montreal, Canada: McGill-Queen's University Press, 2019).
33 Lori Emerson, *Reading Writing Interfaces: From the Digital to the Bookbound* (Minneapolis, MN: University of Minnesota Press, 2014); David Karpf, "Something I No Longer Believe: Is Internet Time Slowing Down?" *Social Media + Society*, July–September 2019, 1–4, https://journals.sagepub.com/doi/pdf/10.1177/2056305119849492.
34 Jan Lauren Boyles and Jared Meisinger, "Automation and Adaptation: Reshaping Journalistic Labor in the Newsroom Library," *Convergence: The International Journal of Research into New Media Technologies* 26, no. 1 (2018): 178–92.
35 Some of this section was originally part of the second chapter, which appeared in the *TMG Journal for Media History* and is republished here with permission.

2 Early development of news sites in the UK and the US in the 1990s[1]

In 2021, looking back at how journalism looked online in the 1990s, with its slow, buzzing dial-up, simplistic graphics made of low-resolution photos (if they were posted at all) and lack of streaming, it might be hard to see the connection to the present, with its TikTok, immersive apps and omnipresent (more or less) Wi-Fi.

And yet, we can still learn a great deal about how online news—as we know it—came to be, starting 25 years ago. Comments, links, home pages and dynamic news reporting via online audio, and even video, most definitely did exist then online on newspaper sites, and would, in time, expand into what we consumed, medium-agnostic, on our smartphones, tablets and other devices. As with any technology, online news was path-dependent, and in this case, particularly cross-national, in this case between the United Kingdom and the US.[2] Transnational, comparative work, especially with media or journalism history, adds important context to national histories of technologies, showing that they are, in fact, embedded in global networks and information flows, but also quite literally connected via infrastructures that include physical transmission (i.e., undersea cables), shipping, mining (for the rare earth metals used for computer components), programming and data storage in the form of server forms.

In May 2001, Ruth Addicott, writing in *The Press Gazette* in the UK, observed that "magazine publishers are beginning to breathe again after years of panic, intimidation and misinformation caused by the impact of the internet."[3] Addicott was paraphrasing an American business leader at a recent meeting of the British Professional Publishers Association, a prominent trade organization for magazines. These kinds of interactions were relatively commonplace, as has been explored by other scholars.[4]

But this summary of a speech about "the hype of the web" is revealing about the many close, still-underexplored, trans-Atlantic connections between the US and Britain. Publishers, software engineers and journalists in both nations shared worries about the impact of the internet on the

DOI: 10.4324/9780429324871-2

newspaper industry, and the early migration—or, in many cases, the uneven migration—to online news sites during the 1990s. This chapter explores some of those shared concerns, down to the editor and reporter level, with a special focus on the mid-to-late 1990s, and concluding with what changed by the end of that decade and what did not. By focusing on the exchange and shared struggle of the US and Great Britain, scholars can better understand the ways both nations' journalism industries reacted to, adapted or failed to adapt to the internet. One of its chief aims is to help debunk the myth that the world of newspapers was somehow obliterated by simplistic, bad choices, including failing to charge for content or in putting its best journalism online. Some of this narrative is grounded in reality, of course, including the loss of classified advertising, the "original sin" of giving away content for free without paying for it, and not embracing mobile devices fast enough, among other supposedly decisive, causal factors.[5] But the larger story is a more nuanced one, with many possible "could-have-beens," to be explored below.

In the US and the United Kingdom, there was early enthusiasm in the respective journalism trade press, but also in more academic circles, about what "going on-line" (in the parlance of the day, the hyphen was often included) promised, and it was mostly good. While there was some concern about the long-term impact on profit margins, most of the stories written by reporters and editors focused on early adopters, experimental methods of online storytelling, and future plans to bring more computer-assisted reporting (CAR) methods to the online space, among other hopeful trends.

By the end of the decade, with the dot-com bubble bursting and the dawn of the 2000s, more skepticism and pronounced concern would creep into narratives about technology and what it was doing and would do to journalism. But in order to better understand our digitally delivered journalism today, it helps to see the long, 30-year arc of development that came before. The 1990s, with its heady mix of both traditional momentum and change, transition and lingering stability from the industrial journalism of the late twentieth century, is worthy of special consideration. A strong comparative element across the US and UK will help to draw out both similarities and differences, and paths not taken in both countries. These included more aggressive efforts to develop internet-based journalism, integrate early online sites better with larger print operations, and embed news workers writing for these sites into more traditional newsroom spaces, instead of isolating them.

It is important to reject teleological, simplistic histories of communication technology (especially a technology such as the internet, composed of numerous other technologies), and to show the complexities of a moment such as that experienced by journalism organizations in the early-to-mid-1990s. At this point, even intelligent, thoughtful people were uncertain as to the next step in the face of disruption and change. An empathetic, cross-national (comparing two countries) media history such as what follows shows that no one country, including and especially the US, exists apart from the rest of the world, and that branching paths and discourse about them show a messy, unclear future, not a preordained, single path. The history of the creation of a commercialized internet, and how news organizations adapted to its possibilities (or not) needs more connected, global accounts, and not just those focused on the US. By looking at how discourse about early sites was mutually shaping on both sides of the Atlantic, this research can make a small, nuanced intervention into received histories of the internet and newspapers, by showing how small, constitutive choices added up, gradually and often in unseen ways, to become the more inevitable-seeming, path-dependent decisions that seem clear in retrospect but which were anything but clear at the moment.

Context: newsroom computerization right before the internet

When Paul Williams wrote his conclusion to *The Computerized Newspaper* in the UK, in 1990, he contemplated what a transition to microcomputers, or personal computers, would mean for journalists in the 1990s. This would be defined by the "fourth wave" of newsroom computerization: "the use of 'standard platforms'—computers . . . that you can buy off the shelf" alongside software systems that you could also buy as-is. This was in contrast to the customized, multimillion-dollar/pound installations by the likes of Raytheon or Digital Equipment Corporation, Systems Integrators Incorporated (SII), Atex, or Hastech, in the UK, specifically.[6] Williams talked about how PCs were becoming the norm in the US, but how there were some differences in the UK. These differences, which are discussed below, show how, despite many cultural and technological parallels, the immediate pre-internet era was experienced differently by newsrooms in Britain than in the US.

In Britain, the main daily paper was likely to be the national or at least regional paper of record (the leading so-called "quality" paper, in the language of British journalism), due to a variety of factors, including the size of the country but also the politicized presence of party-affiliated news. Small papers in Britain were likely truly local—i.e., they could "only dream of the sort of investment that their American cousins can afford, so the introduction of new technology for them must be at a much lower cost." In other words, American newspapers and their owners could afford more readily the expenses required to upgrade their newsrooms and news workers with the latest technology tools. Also, in contrast, in the US, local newspapers were much more distributed, and that also meant that they were more interested in many cases in investing in technology for their workers, individually or as part of chains.[7] Stories from the trade press in the 1980s were replete with tales of cost-effective newsroom computer retrofits.

While the history of newsroom computerization, pre-civilian internet, is worthy of its own story, there were some significant overlaps with pre-internet networks, including legal and other research databases, that distinguished the similar but somewhat divergent paths both nations' newspaper industries took when it came to the development of early news sites.[8] These sites emerged out of an existing computing and network environment that influenced discussion about them and their eventual design. Whether it was through American Online, Prodigy, CompuServe or their emulators in their pioneering use of graphical user interface (GUI) technologies, newspaper sites were rarely built from scratch and instead constructed as part of larger efforts by other companies.

When Williams, for example, notes that few, if any, newspapers had been able to truly move over to an all-PC system, for layout, pagination and text input, he was speaking primarily of the smaller papers in the UK that struggled to save enough money to adopt such systems. And yet, when he discusses the use of early portable modems, or "phone couplers," to transmit early digital images from reporters in the field back to their newsrooms, he could be describing developments in the States. Ultimately, the dream of publishers and owners on both sides of the ocean was similar: "the aim must be to produce one work station that can do the lot, and be integrated with existing databases, maintaining the integrity both of the stories and of the composition." To be clear, at the time, with the possible exception of some customized Apple Macintosh computers, this was still a few years away.[9]

In the British context, there was a long tradition of relying on mainframes or large minicomputers instead of PCs, despite the gradual adoption of IBM machines starting in the 1970s and 1980s. This is explored in detail in Mar Hicks' history of the British computing industry during the Cold War.[10] In the US, there was greater emphasis on decentralized systems, including how workers were hired and trained.[11]

There were attempts—mostly unsuccessful—to emulate the British Prestel videotex system, developed by the Post Office there, and the French Minitel.[12] In the US, this primarily involved the multimillion-dollar Viewtron project by Knight Ridder, which tried—and failed—to recoup a $55 million investment in a pre-internet information service for average Americans.[13] Other systems, such as the Fort Worth, Texas, *Star-Telegram* "Startext" were more successful, on local and regional levels. This study does not explore these related technologies, but the work of other scholars such as Kevin Driscoll does.[14] For our purposes, we will focus on the era from about 1993 through 2001, with a particular emphasis on c. 1995 to about 2000. This was a moment of possibility and change, with long-term consequences for the newspaper industry. Indeed, decisions made then—and not just about the use of paywalls and customized editions online, etc.—continue to reverberate down to our present moment, some 30 years later. By examining this period as a media-historical hinge point, especially in a comparative way, we can understand more of the difficulties of prediction and why proactive responses to disruptive innovation are so challenging.[15]

Understanding "disruption"

Following Valerie Belair-Gagnon and Allison Steinke and their summary of innovation-oriented research in journalism studies, this chapter (and the larger project) is grounded in several theoretical approaches.[16] The first is the older but still useful diffusion-of-innovations, popularized in the mid-twentieth century by historians of technology but especially shaped by Everett Rogers. Eric Schatzberg has outlined a history of the larger debates, including criticisms, around Rogers' influential *Diffusions of Innovations*, published in 1962.[17] This much-discussed theory of technology adoption has an enduring quality, speaking as it does to innovators, early adopters, early majority, late majority and laggards, as "adopter categories." In the classical conception of Rogers' theory, a further five "factors" impact on how innovations are adopted, including relative advantage, compatibility, complexity, triability and observability.[18] It has been criticized for being too linear, not comprehensive and too focused on corporate concerns, versus innovation by amateurs and hobbyists.[19]

I am particularly influenced by how the Spanish media historian Ángel Arrese, in his study of the origin of paywalls, has used this approach, and elaborated on the "retro-innovation" that accompanies discourse about innovation by industry practitioners. This is the process by which past choices are justified through the lens of the present. One could think of it as the "oh, of course that was how things were supposed to happen," argument, which, while greatly simplified, is essentially a presentist perspective that looks at technologies as received versus evolving, or as steady state, as opposed to more fluid.[20] In adopting the latter approach, Arrese is focused on what he describes as the "return to basics of rediscovery of the value of news," in regard to paywalls and subscription models for journalism, within but also without the American context. He examines how the rhetorical and literal (at least in the digital realm) construction of paywalls for the leading publications in France, Spain, Germany, the UK and other European countries, as well as select parts of East Asia, coincided with a move to rebuild the ramparts, so to speak, in the US.[21] He applies Rogers' diffusions theory, which helps to explain how a practice once held as anathema—charging again for access to news, or at least premium news content—was readopted and revalued.

When reading discourse from the 1990s, one can quickly note that the newspaper industry was not caught in some kind of simplistic flat-footedness, or doomed to one direction, and so the diffusions model, while helpful, is not a panacea. While the narratives of adoption, acceptance, rejection, setbacks and success roughly follow the steps outlined by Rogers, there are some critical divergences. The impact of the internet on the newspaper industry and in particular the ways that British and American leading newspapers developed their sites elides, or even resists, an easy explanatory model (not to say that the more evolved version of the diffusion of innovations, focused on a holistic or systems approach, is not sophisticated). In this approach, my work is influenced by Steen Steensen's call for a grounded theory of innovation focused on the power of individual actors within institutions (while not reducing media-history narratives to great-men-and-women tales).[22] Steensen draws on Pablo Boczkowski, who identified three structural factors, including proximity between print and online newsrooms, gatekeeping reproduction, and a view of the audience as consumers or producers.

But he also identifies a fourth factor, namely, the suitability of a technology (or, rather, how "is it suited to fulfill its promise").[23]

Suitability has a slightly esoteric feel, but a respect for users' needs and a practical element are built into this concept, including an awareness of the limitations of certain platforms. In the case of the promise of the internet in opening access to newsrooms for readers, for curating stories that were more interactive and substantive, and not just as adjunct or supplemental, this study takes up this concern raised by Steensen, and responds to his call for applications for grounded theories of innovation. Steensen found in his study of a Norwegian news site that individual actions and cooperation still mattered, and that the multiple, overlapping processes of innovation can be "complex and random due to the unstable structure of online newsrooms." He called on future researchers to contemplate the impact of newsroom autonomy, work culture, management, the relevance (and not just the existence) of new technology tools, and of course those innovative, individual actors.[24]

News websites in the UK in the mid-1990s

When looking at how "home" pages for newspapers were conceived, created and used in the mid-1990s in Britain and the US, it will help to briefly trace the ways these sites appeared in both countries. In his 2001 book on

Figure 2.1 "Weekly runs profitable web site."

Source: Hoag Levins. "Weekly Runs Profitable Web Site." *Editor & Publisher*, December 28, 1996, 26.

the news industry and the internet, British scholar Jim Hall noted that journalism was just the third major global sector, after the military and higher education, to go online. By the late 1990s, both the US and Great Britain had most of their major national papers on the internet in some way, shape or form.[25]

In fact, from 1995 to June 1997, the number of newspapers online grew from as many as 491 to 3,600, with many of these found in either the US or the UK.[26] Other, more conservative estimates put that figure at growing from 50 in 1995 to 5,000 in 1999, with 2,800 in the US.[27] But numbers alone do not tell the full story. The appearance, purpose and actual use of these sites need to be understood in their proper context, along with the motives of those who built them. What follows, then, is not meant to be exhaustive, but is, rather, a brief, historically grounded examination of some of the major trends during the mid-to-late 1990s for news organizations and their moves online. It should be understood at the beginning that "news site" here usually refers to the home pages of newspapers, but also a few (then rare) dedicated online-news operations and their sites.

In Britain, *The Guardian, The Times, The Telegraph* and BBC News were all leaders when it came to getting their journalism online, with the first former under the banner of "Guardian Unlimited." Alan Rusbridger, the editor-in-chief of *The Guardian* for some 20 years beginning in 1995, recounts in his memoir that "reach before revenue" was the dominant model then, for how to develop an online presence, and he honestly recalls, too, the many missteps and accidents along the way. On a fact-finding mission, right before his tenure as the top editor, he visited his American counterparts, seeing firsthand the early efforts being made by *The New York Times, The Atlanta Journal-Constitution* (with its alliance with the Prodigy Online Service), the Knight Ridder laboratory in Boulder, Colorado, run by Roger Fidler, with his ahead-of-their-time, mock-up news tablets, and the *Chicago Tribune*, among other destinations. But this was no mere sightseeing tour. It was part of a long tradition of technology and idea exchange between journalism on both sides of the Atlantic.

In the more immediate sense, though, the trip made an uncertain impression on Rusbridger. Despite his status as an early adopter and even, later, an early majority leader, to borrow again from Rogers' theoretical framework, and Arrese and Steensen's emphasis on individual choices, it is clear that Rusbridger was *unclear* about what to do at a critical point. Looking back from a quarter century, he is right to point out that no one, not even "navigators and pioneers" like Fidler (in other words, innovators), really knew what was going to happen next. There was simply a vague sense that "it would be more reckless not to experiment," and that big and small publishers alike were conflicted on how to proceed with transitioning to online, how fast, and when.[28]

By March 1996, *The Guardian* began to plan its more intentional online launch in earnest, deciding not to charge for its online content, on the presumption that more contact with readers would help advertising and eventually the print product. Even so, the initial amount of money invested was £200,000, a modest sum compared to the £6 million being invested into *The Guardian*'s sister paper, *The Observer*, over three years.[29] This plan would be revised again in 1997, with limited forays online before that, by the paper, during major news events such as the death of Princess Diana on August 31, 1997. In July 1998, six sites, with an additional 12 over the next year and a half, under the broad umbrella of "Guardian Unlimited," brought in an initial 100,000 registered readers (often described as "users"). The "verticals" run by *The Guardian*'s new digital team focused on breaking news, politics, film, sports, books, arts and jobs.

Like other sites during this era, it was mostly text-based, with some lower resolution images, but was pioneering in its use of permanent URLs, forums, and digital photography. Streaming video, which would not emerge until the mid-2000s, was not present. While some video files were included, they took at least several minutes to download and play, and often much longer. But by October 1999, there were some 500,000 registered users, with about 60 news workers, 20 of them being more traditional journalists, dedicated to the site.[30] While it was, in time, quite successful, especially as American readers discovered the site in the wake of 9/11, lingering tensions were present. An academic team looking at the paper in 1998 reported that only a minority of reporters were using the web on a daily basis. Indeed, it took several years for everyone in the main newsroom to gain full access to terminals that let them get online in a more functional way. These were added to the newsroom at a cost of some £3.5 million.[31]

Eventually, under first Ian Katz and then Simon Waldman and Emily Bell, *Guardian* staffers singled out by Rusbridger as important to the success of the site, over the course of its first five years of existence, some £18 million would be spent, with staff costs being among the chief expenditures. While this seems like a great deal of money, Rupert Murdoch would spend some $2 billion on various online efforts which, in contrast, mostly failed spectacularly, between 1999 and 2001.[32] Projections of how much money could be made at the more careful *Guardian* ranged from £8 million to £30 million a year in profits, by 2005, but that was still very much uncertain, something that worried Rusbridger in the midst of the dot-com bubble in the summer of 2000.[33]

Peter Preston, the former editor-in-chief of *The Guardian* before Rusbridger, who had been helping to lead the technology development at *The Guardian* as part of its Product Development Unit, expressed his own skepticism as late as 2007, at a newspaper conference in the UK.

When asked by a colleague about the topic, he said that "he did post work online but never accepted any payment for that work because in his view it did not constitute real journalism. It was shovelware. Overly long, insufficiently well[-]edited, first[-]draft materials. He was not alone in holding these views [sic]."[34] Shovelware, to be clear, was a derogatory term for content posted to the web.[35] While the paper had an additional financial runway, due to its unique ownership model (via The Scott Trust, still supplemented today by donations from readers), the doubt expressed by

Preston and others was not necessarily misplaced. Through the early 2000s, it was not clear if websites, and later a social-media presence, would be as necessary as they seem today for news organizations. They were decidedly still news*papers*, at this point.

Elsewhere in the UK, the launch of BBC News Online in November 1997 was met with initial skepticism, as it was perceived to be "late on the scene, arriving long after both British and international competitors had established their online presence."[36] However, in time, with an investment of some £20 million, BBC News was able to give its 40 dedicated digital journalists the margin they needed to succeed. Relying on its global network of some 2,000 staff, 250 correspondents, along with 13 domestic and 42 international bureaus, it was soon a respected success. Daily video and hourly audio versions (the latter also in Arabic, Cantonese, Mandarin, German, Russian and Spanish) of the *BBC World Service* were popular, especially as leadership opted for less flashy, more robust tools such as RealVideo and RealAudio. It had one million hits on its first day of operation, and more than eight million page impressions a month by March 1998. By June 1998, BBC News had 61,000 individual pages of news content.[37]

The BBC had the advantage of tapping into a deep bench and planetary network, and, of course, was subsidized by a TV licensing fee and an exclusive lock on its customers. It was also, obviously, not a newspaper and thus did not have to grapple with infrastructure concerns to quite the same degree as a print newspaper. For example, while many newspapers had to hire temporary stringers to cover events in the developing world, the BBC would often have a fully staffed news bureau on hand. Nonetheless, like *The Guardian*, the BBC demonstrated an early appetite for trusted news by legacy institutions, despite the popularity of sites such as The Drudge Report in both the US and Britain (Drudge was and remains a kind of curated rumor site, linking to other news sites, and mostly setting a news agenda via its creative use of headlines). The BBC's experience drew on its close watching of its American, corporate equivalents: its online editor, Mark Smartt, had visited CNN and ABC's nascent online operation. Smartt insisted on collaborative efforts with existing TV news staff, and an ethos of multiskilled, digital-friendly journalism was set far sooner than in the US.[38]

As the 2000s dawned, readership from the US helped to swell the numbers of people reading, listening, watching and otherwise consuming online journalism in the UK. Newspapers as diverse as the tabloid *Daily Mail* and the trade publication of record, the *Press Gazette*, transitioned to a more robust online presence.[39]

BBCi CATEGORIES TV RADIO COMMUNICATE WHERE I LIVE INDEX SEARCH Go

BBC NEWS UPDATED EVERY MINUTE OF EVERY DAY

Front Page
World
UK
UK Politics
Business
Sci/Tech
Health
Education
Entertainment
Talking Point
In Depth
AudioVideo

WORLD CUP

BBC SPORT
BBC Weather

SERVICES
Daily E-mail
News Ticker
Mobiles/PDAs

Feedback
Help

Low Graphics

LANGUAGES
NOTICIAS
時事天地
NEWYDDION

Thursday, 30 May, 2002, 03:49 GMT 04:49 UK

Leeds beat Sunderland 2-0 in English Premiership.

West warns of Kashmir war
The US and Britain warn both India and Pakistan that there is a serious danger the Kashmir crisis could spiral into military conflict.

Also:
- The military balance
- Nuclear brinksmanship
- Q&A;: Kashmir dispute

In Depth: Kashmir flashpoint
Talking Point: What action should the world take?

New powers to expel refugees
Thousands of refugees to whom asylum has been denied will be removed from Britain before they can appeal.

Also:
- UK 'to expel Afghan asylum seekers'
- 'No Tory rift' over tough asylum stance
- France aims to shut Sangatte

US welcomes Libya's 'Lockerbie offer'
Libya's reported offer of compensation over the bombing of Pan Am Flight 103 is described as a "step in the right direction" by the US.

Also:
- Gaddafi re-emerges
- Families cautious
- Long search for the truth

Hit squads for social services
Private sector trouble-shooters will be sent in to rescue social services in four local authority areas in England.

FBI unveils major shake-up
The FBI announces sweeping reforms in response to criticism over its role both before and after the attacks of 11 September.

AROUND THE WORLD NOW
AFRICA EUROPE

WATCH/LISTEN
BULLETINS ON DEMAND
BBC Radio latest
BBC News 24
BBC World Service radio
BBC One TV news
LIVE AND COMING UP
0445GMT/0545BST
World Cup England news conference
VIDEO CHOICE
A "symbolic closure" for Ground Zero
- Programme pages

LAUNCH CONSOLE FOR LATEST AUDIO/VIDEO

IN DEPTH
Golden Jubilee
Full coverage of the Queen's celebration

TALKING POINT
Fifa vote
Your views on Blatter's re-election

Race UK
Angry young men

How to be fish-friendly

QUESTION TIME
VOTE
You shape the debate

WORLD CUP
E-MAIL SERVICES
Get your team's news

Famine warning
UN confirms 10 million southern Africans at risk

Hawking jets
The UK warplane

1/3

Figure 2.2 BBC News' home page, May 30, 2003.

Source: BBC News' home page, on May 30, 2003; accessed via the Internet Archive's Wayback Machine, September 15, 2021, https://web.archive.org/web/20020530041546/http://news.bbc.co.uk/

News websites in the US in the mid-1990s

In the US, online news, too, grew in popularity in similar fits and starts. Bruce Garrison, writing in 2005, noted that by the end of 1996, more than 800 news sites of some kind or another existed, with many of these static or secondary, but still established, and with 1,600 worldwide. "Newspapers, more than any other medium, raced to go online during the mid-1990s," spurred on, as Stuart Allan observed, by big news events, such as the 1995 Oklahoma City bombing, the second term of President Bill Clinton, with its various scandals, and the sad fate of Princess Diana, all of which fascinated Americans.[40]

But a much-smaller subgroup of news sites and their parent papers—early adopters—remained active and innovative. Publishers were worried about the still-niche market for the internet, and about competing with their print product. Looking back, this may seem foolish, but from their perspective, the paper paid the bills, and internet users numbered, at most, in the hundreds of thousands, not yet the billions of the twenty-first century.

Among others, *The Washington Post*, *San Jose Mercury News*, *Boston Globe*, *New York Times*, *Chicago Tribune*, *Dallas Morning News*, *Los Angeles Times*, *Miami Herald*, *USA Today* and *Wall Street Journal* stood out in Garrison's estimation. Whether because they were among the first to post original content online, like the *Mercury News*, which considered itself the authoritative journalistic voice for Silicon Valley, or broke scoops (news reported nowhere else), like the *Morning News*, or had committed corporate backing, like the *Herald*, an early paywall, like the *Wall Street Journal*, or, in the case of the *Tribune*, a partnership with a pioneering and popular graphical user interface (GUI) and web provider such as America Online, these news organizations distinguished themselves early in the American context for taking risks and investing in an unproven technology.[41]

Generally, though, then as now, the lack of a consistently successful business model eluded publishers. Following the broad British idea of trying for technical feasibility and audience first, and profit later, few of these sites dared to charge for their content, sometimes called the "original sin" of online journalism, as referenced earlier.[42] A variety of "online news service models" were proposed, in the absence of a clear contender. These models included:

- 24-hours-a-day continuous news (such as CNN or later, Fox News)
- community bulletin board (essentially a static host site for forums)
- supplementary news site (special one-off sites covering events such as the 1996 Olympics)
- exclusive news site (focused on breaking news)[43]

Other models projected that news sites might go more "mainstream," evolve into "index and category," "meta and comment" or "share and discussion" formats, or assume some other, as-yet undetermined form.[44] By the late 2000s, most newspapers would realize that they were losing far too much money, and having to invest far too many resources, in terms of sustainably maintaining profit margins, at least, to give away all their content all the time, and attempted paywalls, something the industry is still transitioning to today. Early paywalls mostly did not work, or at least not very well.

Any massive shift away from advertising and (back) to subscribers was still some time away, and online news as an adjunct, or secondary medium, would define the era in the US for most news organizations.

Nonetheless, tools such as news blogs, live interviews with experts, linking and the deployment of video and audio would, as in the UK, mean that newspapers were no slouches when it came to trying out storytelling on the internet. Challenges for the industry included the creation of reliable and relatively easy-to-use content management systems, digital photography and, in the larger marketplace, the gradual replacement of "dial-up" internet with faster broadband.[45] Journalists also faced deskilling, reskilling or at best, uneven workflows with digital tools, leading to a debate by the mid-2000s by both practitioners and scholars about the kinds of affordances that could be attributed to online-news tech, if any.[46]

Before all this, however, the overall feeling in the American journalism trade literature was one of optimism—news sites would lead to better reporting, a tighter bond with readers and a way to finally regain some of the breaking news edges lost long ago to TV and radio news.

"Nobody sees the death of the ink and paper newspaper," wrote Jack Lail in the winter 1994 issue of the Society of Professional Journalists' *Quill*. "Electronic newspapers can be painfully slow on services that charge by the minute [a common practice at the time]. Generally, they lack photos, graphics and video, and don't have the carry-it-anywhere portability of the good old newspaper."[47]

And yet, especially at field-leading newspapers such as the *San Jose Mercury News*, and its "Mercury Center" (the name of its web-based edition, much like Guardian Unlimited), there was hope that readers would "send letters to editors, join group chats with newspaper personalities, read classified ads, search its library, and discuss with each other everything from bike trails to foreign affairs."[48] At "Chicago Online," the *Chicago Tribune*'s online portal powered by AOL, users could buy tickets to see the Chicago Bulls or go to a concert. Still, management believed it was a kind of experiment and not a replacement for their primary product.[49]

This idea of "interactive newspapers" inspired a special section of the leading American trade journal on the news industry, *Editor & Publisher*, in February 1995. But even in this early excitement, some voices expressed concern. At least one observer wrote that the difference between 1990 and 1995, with the commercial internet ascendant, was that "the world has become a tangled web," no longer just "the internet," but a place where users expected a much richer, real-time experience than many newspapers had prepared for. With this "Web/Mosaic environment [a reference to a popular early GUI], the hierarchy of information provision has been turned on its head," with no need for an all-knowing, single source of news, wrote one observer.[50] Others remained hopeful, that, in time, even—and perhaps especially—smaller newspapers could effectively launch and maintain attractive sites for their readers.[51]

At the end of the decade, with the proliferation of dedicated online news sites, a special issue of *Columbia Journalism Review* was still mostly full of optimistic projections about what the 2000s would bring to online news in the US. Frank Houston, a thoughtful analyst, reminded readers that the "web," i.e., the easier way of getting around on the internet, was still very, very young. He pointed to the launches of websites such as Slate and Salon, in 1996 and 1995, respectively, as indicative of the promise for niche sites for commentary on culture and technology, among other topics.[52]

After the terrorist attacks of September 11, 2001, many readers felt the need for better, faster, more in-depth online news—this kind of web-based news would move decidedly from a novelty to a necessity, though the full story of that is beyond the scope of this short study.[53]

The end of the beginning: how the US and UK experiences were similar . . . and different

The era was marked by a sharp divide between those in favor of moving more news online, with the accompanying affordances that would bring, and those who wanted to invest more heavily in print.[54]

Rusbridger noted that even as 9/11 and other seismic news events of the late 1990s and early 2000s demonstrated a hunger for trusted news organizations like newspapers to shift coverage to the internet, his colleagues—and even himself, at times—questioned the viability of doing so. Alongside these growing anxieties, though, the *Guardian*'s Unlimited site, and its peers such as BBC Online, gained popularity.

"Many colleagues were binary—understandably suspicious," he wrote. "If you loved digital then you must hate print, right? What was wrong with print? It still paid our wages—unlike digital pipe dreams. It had serendipity and portability—and generated cash."[55] He would explain that while he still adored print, and had spent his whole career up to that point primarily in that medium, that "loving one didn't mean hating the other. In the end the choice would be out of our hands."[56]

These concerns, and a gradual, emergent strain of worry, appeared in the American trade press. Jerry Ceppos, a retired Knight Ridder executive and the former dean of the Manship School of Mass Communication at Louisiana State University, recalled that his company, then among the larger newspaper chains in the world, was heavily invested in research and development with the internet. But it was hard—actually, nearly impossible, to see where things were going next, even at the end of the decade.

He recalled that the fate of classified-ad advertising, later consumed by the likes of Craigslist, but also job-hunting sites such as Monster.com or LinkedIn, worried his peers, keeping some literally awake at night. While it is too simplistic of a tale to lay the whole blame of the news industry's troubles at the fate of Craig Newmark, the founder of Craigslist, as other scholars and journalism observers have rightly demonstrated, it is just one example of the many unknowns faced by the newspaper world's leaders in the US as well as the UK.[57]

Other observers from the end of this Web 1.0 era were concerned *and* hopeful about what internet technologies could do with journalism. Journalists were no different than any other white-collar occupational group of that era when it came to having mixed feelings. "Reporters still go out on assignment and do investigative work, but they are more selective, especially since technology has added chores once done in composing rooms and control booths," noted Michael Bugeja in *Quill* in May 2005.[58]

Bugeja, who at the time was the director of the Greenlee School of Journalism and Communication at Iowa State University, was worried that "the cumulative effect of greed, downsizing and computerization eventually may create an investigative void in a republic with a free press founded on the principle that truth, not profit, should rise to the top so that voters can make informed choices." In some ways, though, Bugeja's more pessimistic strain remained in the minority. And it should be noted that in previous generations, reporters were discouraged from using telephones, for fear that doing so would keep them confined to their offices.[59]

Other, more positive views from this era noted innovations such as the vertical news blog, with reporters posting their raw notes and files to their own personal or professional sites, with or without official blessing from their news organizations, but also the use of early streaming videos. In an ad from the spring 2000 issue of *Columbia Journalism Review*, for example, the Associated Press announced its partnership with Real Networks for "AP Streaming News."

"For news that words alone cannot deliver, AP brings you real-time sound and video of the day's top stories," the ad promised, along with easy embedding on news sites. The idea behind streaming video was to provide cable-news production values with a deeper network of reports and experts. While not quite a dead end, it was not until most news consumers adopted faster internet connections a few years later that this kind of streaming news video became viable.[60]

Conclusion

When thinking about how parallel progress, however uneven, was made toward the launch of an early experimentation with online news in both the UK and the US in the 1990s, it is critical to think about paths not taken, or the lost potential of joint projects. One wonders what would have become of more collaboration between, let us say, *The Washington Post* and *The Guardian*, or *The Times* of London and *The New York Times*, more than a decade before WikiLeaks. There were early experiments in the 2000s, but most did not go beyond informal proposals.

There were technical and cultural hurdles for concerned group efforts to get online as an industry, some of which will be discussed in the next chapter. For the US–UK collaborations of the 1990s, these included a lack of high-speed internet adoption in both countries and the more politicized nature of news in the UK. But even so, there were far more similarities, then as now, than differences between the two nation's media systems. The potential for co-development was there, at least as revealed in the discourse in journalistic trade publications from this era. In the broader sense, and contrary to popular myths, many news organizations were *not* caught off guard, overwhelmed or necessarily too slow to adapt to the internet. As this chapter has shown, many publishers in both the UK and the US were indeed information-society pioneers, data-driven, overly cautious at times, perhaps, but aware of the big changes about to wash over the world due to the internet.

They, in fact, led the way with vetted news online, long before Apple, Google, Facebook, Amazon and Microsoft became aware of, or concerned about, such things. There is a further danger of treating technology adoption as a kind of universal process, replacing the need for case-based, granular histories. This has happened in media histories for pre-internet analog computing machines and related technologies involving "legacy systems."[61] But by utilizing a diffusions-of-innovations approach, and embracing, instead of pushing aside, the complexity of contingency, this study and others like it can contribute to a deeper appreciation of the messiness and uncertainty of particular historical moments. This kind of transitionary moment occurred in the 1990s with the emergence of news sites. It may be happening again with the rise of virtual reality and related tools for digital storytelling. But we may not know that for another generation. Let us hope that future media historians can take a similarly nuanced view of change in our own era.[62]

When looking at the 1990s and early 2000s, therefore, and at how national contexts impacted both the development of online news, but also how figures such as Rusbridger and Fidler encountered and influenced each other, it is fair to say that the adoption of the internet by news organizations was fraught, connected, and conditional. It was fraught, in being a moment full of promise but also one with largely unproven technologies and business models, connected, in being a time when companies were emerging from a post-Cold War context and thus with their global economic fates more interwoven than before, and conditional, in that media companies had the resources to invest in new technologies, but were cautious, reflexively, about what to do with those same resources.

These contingent networks would lead, in time, to more formal collaborations, including story and resource sharing, with big stories such as political corruption and global pandemics. And it is these ties that may bring some hope for journalism as it continues to adapt to the economics of the online world. Arguably, the ongoing survival of journalism on both sides of the Atlantic is intrinsically linked, and has been so, since before the dawn of the internet age.

The next chapter explores some large-scale reactions to the internet by the newspaper industry in the US.

Notes

1 This chapter first appeared in slightly modified form in the *TMG Journal for Media History*, published by the Netherlands Institute for Sound and Vision, in fall 2021; it is reused here with permission; see Will Mari, "Early Development of News Sites in the United Kingdom and the United States in the 1990s: Exploring Trans-Atlantic Connections," *TMG Journal for Media History*, www.tmgonline.nl/.

2 Cross-national research looks at two nations, and transnational research tends to examine two or more national contexts, but I will use the two terms fairly interchangeably here.

3 Ruth Addicott, "Magazines Back on Track After Net Panic," *Press Gazette*, May 3, 2001, www.pressgazette.co.uk/magazines-back-on-track-after-net-panic/.

4 See, for example, Jeremy Tunstall, *The Media Were American: U.S. Mass Media in Decline*. 2nd ed. (New York: Oxford University Press, 2007).

5 Ethan Zuckerman, "The Internet's Original Sin It's Not Too Late to Ditch the Ad-Based Business Model and Build a Better Web," *The Atlantic*, August 14, 2014, www.theatlantic.com/technology/archive/2014/08/advertising-is-the-internets-original-sin/376041/.

6 Paul Williams, *The Computerized Newspaper: A Practical Guide for Systems Users* (Oxford: Heinemann Professional Publishing Ltd., 1990), 15, 283.

7 Ibid., 285.

8 Will Mari, *A Short History of Disruptive Journalism Technologies* (Abingdon, UK: Routledge, 2019).
9 Williams, *Computerized Newspaper*, 287.
10 Mar Hicks, *Programmed Inequality: How Britain Discarded Women Technologists and Lost Its Edge in Computing.* (Cambridge, MA: MIT Press, 2017).
11 Mari, *A Short History of Disruptive Journalism Technologies.*
12 Julien Mailland and Kevin Driscoll, *Minitel: Welcome to the Internet* (Cambridge, MA: MIT Press, 2017).
13 David Carlson, "The History of Online Journalism," in *Digital Journalism: Emerging Media and the Changing Horizons of Journalism*, ed. Kevin Kawamoto (Lanham, MD: Rowan & Littlefield, 2003), 31–55.
14 Kevin Driscoll, "Hobbyist Inter-Networking and the Popular Internet Imaginary: Forgotten Histories of Networked Personal Computing, 1978–1998" (PhD dissertation, University of Southern California, 2015).
15 For a collection of oral histories from this era, see Michael Shapiro, Anna Hiatt, and Mike Hoyt, *Tales from the Great Disruption: Insights and Lessons from Journalism's Technological Transformation* (Minneapolis, MN: Big Roundtable Books, 2015).
16 Valerie Belair-Gagnon and Allison J. Steinke, "Capturing Digital News Innovation Research in Organizations, 1990–2018," *Journalism Studies* 21, no. 12 (2020): 1724–43. They conclude that while perhaps underutilized, a diffusions-of-innovation approach has a rich legacy in journalism studies and encourages a historical grounding for its (and other theoretical) application(s), following the work of Margaret H. DeFleur and Lucinda D. Davenport; see their, "Innovation Lag: Computer-Assisted Classrooms vs. Newsrooms," *The Journalism Educator* 48, no. 2 (1993): 26–36.
17 Everett Rogers, *Diffusion of Innovations*. 4th ed. (New York: Free Press, 1995); Eric Schatzberg, "Where Do Models of Innovation Come from? Benoit Godin, *Models of Innovation*," *Technology and Culture* 61, no. 1 (2020): 337–40; Benoit Godin, *Models of Innovation: The History of an Idea* (Cambridge, MA: MIT Press, 2017).
18 See Wayne W. LaMorte, "Diffusion of Innovation Theory," *Behavioral Change Models, Boston University School of Public Health*, accessed March 10, 2021, https://sphweb.bumc.bu.edu/otlt/mph-modules/sb/behavioralchangetheories/behavioralchangetheories4.html; see also Leif Singer, "On the Diffusion of Innovations: How New Ideas Spread," accessed March 10, 2021, https://leif.me/on-the-diffusion-of-innovations-how-new-ideas-spread/.
19 Schatzberg, "Where Do Models of Innovation Come from?" 339; Schatzberg gives Rupert Maclaurin credit for actually originating much of what would become the "linear model" of adoption.
20 Ángel Arrese, "From Gratis to Paywalls: A Brief History of a Retro-Innovation in the Press's Business," *Journalism Studies* 17, no. 8 (2016): 1051–67.
21 Ibid., 1052–53.
22 Steen Steensen, "WHAT'S STOPPING THEM? Towards a Grounded Theory of Innovation in Online Journalism," *Journalism Studies* 10, no. 6 (2009): 821–36.
23 Pablo Boczkowski, *Digitizing the News: Innovation in Online Newspapers* (Cambridge, MA: MIT Press, 2004); Steensen, "WHAT'S STOPPING THEM?" 824–25.
24 Steensen, "WHAT'S STOPPING THEM?" 832–33.
25 Jim Hall, *Online Journalism: A Critical Primer* (London: Pluto Press, 2001), 3.

26 Alan Rusbridger, *Breaking News: The Remaking of Journalism and Why It Matters Now* (New York: Picador, 2017), 24. Some scholars, including Christine Ogan and Randy Beam, have a modest estimate of these sites, probably more "truly" dedicated to hosting news content, with as few as a few dozen, about 60, and no more than about 500. In any case, throughout the 1990s, the number of newspaper web sites on both sides of the Atlantic would grow substantially. The quality of the sites, of course, would vary, from a static web page for a smaller newspaper to a dedicated, separate operation like that used for *The Guardian* or *The San Jose Mercury News* and the latter's Mercury Center. For more on Mercury Center, see Michael Shapiro's oral history, "The Newspaper That Almost Seized the Future," *The Columbia Journalism Review*, November–December 2011, https://archives.cjr.org/feature/the_newspaper_that_almost_seized_the_future.php; see also Christine Ogan and Randy Beam, "Internet Challenges for Media Businesses," in *The Internet and American Business*, eds. William Aspray and Paul Ceruzzi (Cambridge, MA: MIT Press, 2008), 279–314.

27 Arrese, "From Gratis to Paywalls." Arrese, in turn, draws from Chip Brown, "State of the American Newspaper. Fear.com," *American Journalism Review* 20, no. 10 (1999): 50–71.

28 Rusbridger, *Breaking News*, 28–29.

29 Ibid., 47.

30 Ibid., 58–61.

31 Ibid., 73.

32 Ibid., 57, 64–65.

33 Ibid., 65.

34 This is a paraphrase of a colleague of Preston's who witnessed his plenary speech at the inaugural Future of Newspapers conference in Cardiff, UK, and had informal conversations with Preston while there. The colleague wished to remain anonymous for this project. For more on Preston, see David McKie, "Peter Preston Obituary: Guardian Editor Who During 20 Years in the Role Played a Decisive Part in Shaping the Paper's Future," *The Guardian*, January 7, 2018, www.theguardian.com/media/2018/jan/07/peter-preston-obituary.

35 "Shovelware," PCMag Encyclopedia, *PC Magazine*, accessed March 11, 2021, www.pcmag.com/encyclopedia/term/shovelware.

36 Stuart Allan, *Online News: Journalism and the Internet* (Berkshire, UK: Open University Press, 2005), 35.

37 Ibid., 36–37.

38 Ibid., 37–38.

39 William Turvill, "Piers Morgan 'Resigns' and Six-Strong Team Launches Website for Daily Mail: Ten Years Ago This Week," *Press Gazette*, May 14, 2014, www.pressgazette.co.uk/piers-morgan-resigns-and-six-strong-team-launches-website-for-daily-mail-ten-years-ago-this-week/; Press Gazette staff, "Our New Website: Cleaner, Quicker and Easier to Use," *Press Gazette*, May 21, 2007, www.pressgazette.co.uk/our-new-website-cleaner-quicker-and-easier-to-use/.

40 Bruce Garrison, "Online Newspapers," in *Online News and the Public*, eds. Michael B. Salwen, et al. (Mahwah, NJ: Lawrence Erlbaum Associations, Publishers, 2005), 3–46, 6; Allan, *Online News*, 2005.

41 Garrison, "Online Newspapers," 20–41.

42 Rusbridger, *Breaking News*, 76; Rusbridger credits media-economics expert Alan Mutter with explicating this phrase; see Ryan Chittum, "Audit Interview:

Alan D. Mutter," *Columbia Journalism Review*, January 23, 2009, https://archives.cjr.org/the_audit/audit_interview_alan_d_mutter_1.php.
43 Garrison, "Online Newspapers," 15–17.
44 Mark Deuze, "Online Journalism: Modeling the First Generation of New Media on the World Wide Web," *First Monday*, November 17, 2003, https://firstmonday.org/article/view/893/802.
45 Juliette De Maeyer. "Content Management Systems and Journalism," *Oxford Research Encyclopedia of Communication*. June 25, 2019, https://oxfordre.com/communication/view/10.1093/acrefore/9780190228613.001.0001/acrefore-9780190228613-e-792.
46 Henrik Örnebring, "Technology and Journalism-as-labor: Historical Perspectives," *Journalism* 11, no. 57 (2010).
47 Jack Lail, "Newspapers On-line: Electronic Delivery Is Hot . . . Again," *Quill*, January–February 1994, 39.
48 Ibid., 40.
49 Ibid., 41.
50 Michael Conniff, "A Tangled Web for Newspapers," *Editor & Publisher*, February 4, 1995, 4–5.
51 Jack Dale, "Real Life Implementation of an Online Newspaper Presence," *Editor & Publisher*, February 4, 1995, 22–24.
52 Frank Houston, "Enjoy the Ride While It Lasts," *Columbia Journalism Review*, July–August 2000, 22–25.
53 To that end, the author is working on a longer, book-length study of the impact of internet on the news industries in the US, UK and Canada, from about 1992 to 2008.
54 An affordance is "the type of action or a characteristic of actions that a technology enables through its design." See Jennifer Earl and Katrina Kimport, *Digitally Enabled Social Change: Activism in the Internet Age* (Cambridge, MA: MIT Press, 2011), 10. See also Peter Preston, who elaborated on some of these issues in, "The Curse of Introversion," in *The Future of Newspapers*, ed. Bob Franklin (London: Routledge, 2009), 13–21.
55 Rusbridger, *Breaking News*, 74.
56 Ibid.
57 Interview with author, June 10, 2020; Ceppos was interviewed as he was a key eyewitness to high-level discussions within Knight Ridder, especially at *The San Jose Mercury News*, where he was managing editor, eventually its executive editor, and responsible for some of the c. 1995-era success of the paper's online news presence, the Mercury Center; see also Shapiro, "The Newspaper That Almost Seized the Future," 63, but also, Jack Shafer, "Don't Blame Craigslist for the Decline of Newspapers: It's Fun to Beat Up on Craig Newmark for the End of Classifieds, but Papers Were Greedy, Too," *Politico*, December 13, 2016, www.politico.com/magazine/story/2016/12/craigslist-newspapers-decline-classifieds-214525; David Streitfeld, "Craig Newmark, Newspaper Villain, Is Working to Save Journalism," *The New York Times*, October 17, 2018, www.nytimes.com/2018/10/17/technology/craig-newmark-journalism-gifts.html.
58 Michael Bugeja, "Computers Keep Reporters in the Office, Off Their Beats," *The Quill*, May 2, 2005, www.quillmag.com/2005/05/02/computers-keep-reporters-in-the-office-off-their-beats/.
59 Will Mari, "Technology in the Newsroom: Adoption of the Telephone and the Radio Car from c. 1920 to 1960," *Journalism Studies* 19, no. 9 (2018), 1366–89.

60 Associated Press and RealNetworks, "AP Streaming News with RealNetworks," *Columbia Journalism Review*, March–April 2000, 1.

61 Leslie Christopher, "As We Could Have Thought: Deploying Historical Narratives of the Memex in Support of Innovation," *Technology and Culture* 61, no. 2 (2020): 480–511; Michael Stevenson and Anne Helmond, "Legacy Systems: Internet Histories of the Abandoned, Discontinued and Forgotten," *Internet Histories* 4, no. 1 (2020): 1–5.

62 To that end, I would recommend the work of David Karpf and Jessa Lingel.

3 The New Century Network and other large-scale industry responses to the internet's arrival

One of the more consistent misnomers about the various ways the newspaper industry in North American and the UK responded to the rise of the internet is that they did basically nothing, at least nothing large-scale, in response to the more immediate threats it brought to their business model. Those threats centered around the narrative of the loss of classified ads (versus other kinds of advertising, which managed to linger longer).

In this version of events, the big players, especially the chains such as Knight Ridder and McClatchy, were caught flat-footed, responded too late, or even not at all. Of course, history is a bit more complex than that, and such is the case here, as this chapter will explore, building off the important work of scholars such as Jessa Lingel, Christine Ogan and Randy Beam.

This chapter highlights some of the larger-scale responses to the internet, including efforts to protect online ads proactively, as well as put these projects into context. Subsequent chapters will look at how these initiatives played out in newsrooms in the form of reporting practices, but also debates about online ethics and the role of online news.

Thinking about the larger milieu will help us understand why, for example, Microsoft was considered a more existential threat than Craigslist (though that perception would flip). Throughout this short book, however, it is important to retain a healthy appreciation for the fog of, if not war, then at least early online business, where the most profitable thing to do was not always apparent.

Context for the creation of the New Century Network: the early fight for online ads

Beginning with informal talks in 1994 that led to a more formal agreement in 1995, the New Century Network (NCN), a coalition of large newspaper companies that tried to develop and protect an increasingly vulnerable

DOI: 10.4324/9780429324871-3

online ad market, found itself shut down just three years later, in early 1998.[1] The NCN was a coalition effort, and thus prone to issues that come from too many processes in parallel versus one effort in unison.

But its existence alone—as flawed as it may have been, for other reasons that will be discussed below—helps to complicate the story of an industry that supposedly did nothing to fight its fate.

The NCN, when it was first launched in the late spring of 1995, had as its initial (albeit somewhat lofty) goal a plan to create 75 newspaper web sites for its various clients, with about 35 planned by the early summer. The network included as its founding partners some of the most successful and well-resourced media corporations in North America at the time, including Knight Ridder, Advance Publications, Cox Newspapers, Gannett, Hearst, Times-Mirror Co., Tribune Co., the Washington Post Co. and the New York Times Co., with each contributing $1 million in seed money.[2] Some of these already had experience developing an online presence, especially Knight Ridder and *The Washington Post*'s parent company, but also Tribune, with its pioneering partnership with AOL.

Editor & Publisher proclaimed the NCN's launch in a May 1995 editorial as a positive move for the industry, as it often did with similar, more independent efforts. The move to share both online ads and also news content was thought to be important. But even the usually supportive *Editor & Publisher* had some initial doubts; for one thing, noted the anonymous editors who celebrated the start of the NCN, there was a potential conflict between the NCN and the Associated Press and its AdSEND service.[3] How the various efforts to stave off online advertisers would work, at least in a unified way, was an open question.

Other early observers, including Katherine Fulton, writing for the *Columbia Journalism Review*, noted the potential for "support [for] local newspapers in providing and sharing on-line content" with the project, comparing it to "Infinet, a joint Knight-Ridder/Landmark Communications project to offer internet access in local communities across the country . . . and new journalistic umbrellas such as the Raleigh *News & Observer*'s Nando.net."[4]

It is important to think of the NCN in the context of anxiety not so much over Craigslist, or other start-ups (recall that Amazon was just barely out of its garage in Washington state, in the US at the time), but in the midst of worry about larger players such as Microsoft and Yahoo!, and not Google, but rather Microsoft's *Slate*, and the Apple-founded *Salon*, online magazines, and Microsoft's network of entertainment guides.

And again, when Knight Ridder and its partners each invested about $1 million in the effort, the NCN was more of a just-in-case bet, and not so much an all-in effort designed for survival—even the savviest prognosticators struggled to imagine scenarios in which the industry would become totally unmoored from its basic, ad-driven business model. It is far easier for us in the 2020s to *see* this than it was for our forebears in the early- to mid-1990s to *imagine* this.

As has been discussed in the previous chapter, the number and capacities of early internet sites, as well as their initial online rivals for classifieds, were limited.[5] And the role of Craigslist as an industry-killer has been grossly exaggerated, as Jessa Lingel outlines in her book on the history and cultural impact of the site. She points out that disruption (both as a theory and as a kind of practice) was then and still is often held up as a kind of virtue, or even an "ethos," in the world of technology start-ups. Disruption is often thus misunderstood as a catch-all, explanatory force for how change impacts established industries. At worst, "disruption" is a kind of panacea—praised as a virtue while unexamined as a concept. But following Lingel's lead, any serious conceptualization of "disruption" should avoid lazy stereotypes, and instead lean into its complexities, as this study attempts to do here.[6]

As has been discussed earlier, classified ads *were* a major source of funding for the newspaper industry, accounting for up to 25 percent of all revenue in the late 1970s, with a 20 percent loss by 2004, and 40 percent in job ads, formerly one of the most popular kinds of classified ads.[7] That meant that the arrival of Craigslist in particular (though it had many imitators, eventually, including efforts by the newspaper industry), "symbolized an upheaval in how people read the news, got information, and connected to their neighborhoods."[8]

Ultimately, she points out, "the blame game of who killed traditional newspapers is based on having clear-cut heroes (local newspapers) and villains (craigslist). But socio-technical shifts in power and influence rarely unfold in straightforward, linear paths."[9]

By way of a helpful example, she highlights how Autotrader, an early entrant (established by the end of the 1990s) in the online car-selling-and-buying world, was and remains owned by Cox Enterprises, a newspaper publisher.[10] Similarly, CareerBuilder, another early effort online, had its roots in a joint effort by Knight Ridder and the Tribune Co. Its predecessor began in 1995, before Monster.com and its copycats.[11] Careerpath was another pioneer, offering job classifieds, and was founded in the fall of 1995 by the *Boston Globe*, the *Chicago Tribune*, the *Los Angeles Tribune*, the *San Jose Mercury News* and the *Washington Post*, and by the end of 1996, some 26 newspapers were posting 150,000 jobs there. Similarly, an effort by the Times Mirror, the Tribune Corporation, and the Washington Post Corporation, Classified Ventures, focused on selling cars and property, with some 150 affiliates in 34 of the top 50 markets by the late summer of 1998.[12] Other business enterprises now thought unique to internet companies such as Google and Amazon had roots in pioneering initiatives by newspaper companies and their partners, including the use of more subtle metrics for web traffic, buying and selling tickets to live entertainment, search engines, online archives, public records portals, online shopping and more.[13]

A Lingel puts it, "any argument that blames online classifieds sites for diminishing newspaper profits must take into account the complex economies of media industries." Classified ads have long been a contested space, she argues, a kind of contested text, in fact, with what is and is not OK to buy and sell. They have also been open (or at least more open than traditional forums) to people on the periphery, outside of the traditional power structures of print publishing.[14] And yet the durability of Craigslist-killing newspapers persists, as a myth.

Part of the reason here is that myths have a kind of utility, providing comfort through familiar, even ritualized narratives. For a field that is already hardwired to receive and reinforce myths, the simplified version of events with online ads provides a kind of satisfying loop.[15] This history of the NCN follows Lingel's example in showing the messy complexities of the mid-1990s internet economy, a daunting unknown for many otherwise savvy media companies.

The NCN's (wobbly) rise

One 1997 prediction called for a $14 billion market by 2000, for online businesses focused on information, up from $5 billion in 1995, with internet ad spending rocketing to $300 million by the end of 1996. That same prediction pointed to 1996 as a turning point, the year that "that internet advertising became an actual business," according to Evan Neufeld, who worked for a consulting firm called Jupiter Communications. This company marketed AdSpend, a tool for tracking the value of internet ads, and so they were invested in this rosy prophecy. Still, the idea that internet ad spending itself could hit up to $5 billion by 2000 was not *entirely* farfetched, as total ad spending was expected to reach as high as $47 billion.[16]

Other industry observers were a bit more circumspect, pointing out that more than 90 percent of the then 800 or so newspapers web sites had not been profitable, as of 1996. With some exceptions, including Boston.com and the Mercury Center, one analyst noted that there was, "a sharp drop off everywhere else. The local newspaper Web sites just aren't getting the traffic or the ads yet. They're not attracting the national advertisers and they're not picking up significant amounts of local advertisers." The ability of display ads, sometimes called banner ads, online, to attract and retain the interest of a healthy cross-section of companies was not guaranteed.[17]

Another factor in the move to protect online advertising pre-emptively was the reluctance to move online at all, beyond a static placeholder page with contact information for the newsroom. While some 1,600 or newspapers were online worldwide in early 1997, according to one estimate, there was still a substantial number that hesitated, due to a lack of resources, including staff and funding, ownership and management changes, or just concerns "about whether the internet and its graphical offspring, the World Wide Web, will add to the bottom line or simply bleed resources that could better be used elsewhere." At one Thomson-owned paper in Mesa, Arizona, the *Tribune*, a move from its previous owners had slowed things down. The paper's managing editor, Jim Ripley, said that any future effort would have to be more creative than just an imitation of the paper version: "Maybe I'm of the wrong generation on that score, but I find it rather tedious to read long things on the Internet, so my personal opinion is that it's a mistake just to replicate the newspaper."[18]

Even in specific efforts to reinforce help-wanted ads online, for example, an established player like the *San Jose Mercury News* and its Mercury Center was not always sure how to proceed.[19] Some experts believed that newspapers could lean into being trusted brands, but had a habit of being slow to act, and even being arrogant with the belief that they knew their local communities better than anyone else.[20]

Newspaper sites also tended not to use content outside of their own operations (and then, as discussed in the second chapter, tended to reuse old content or put up "shovelware"—that unoriginal just-because content), with one survey from early 1997 finding that most sites had some 80 percent of their online material originating from within (so a decidedly uneven use of news-wire copy, for example). The vast majority of papers gave away their content for free, or nearly 90 percent.[21] Many of these sites, often discussed internally still as "projects," were decidedly not profitable. Many newsroom leaders—some 85 percent, in the same survey—said they did not plan on charging for access in the near future, and with the typical staff support for an online news operation consisting of one ad person, one tech person, and two editorial people.[22]

By April 1997, the NCN was attempting to venture into (very limited) aggregated sports content, in this case covering the Triple Crown race, and with its network of papers expanding to about 75, in this case including reporting by the *Lexington Herald-Leader*, the Baltimore *Sun* and the Newark *Star-Ledger*.[23] That summer, the NCN, at least in theory, had grown to 130 sites, 110 of which were being given expanded search capacity. As one report claimed, "In effect, this turns the entire NCN network into a single online publication," though how that functioned was unclear.[24]

Figure 3.1 "The news . . . The online news"[25]

Source: "The News . . . The Online News." *Editor & Publisher*, December 2, 1995, 4.

A further complication was the tendency of the more capable members of the NCN to strike out on their own, with their own initiatives. They remained nominally part of the network, but invested personnel, funding and other forms of capital into what were, in effect, social ventures. These arguably drained the NCN of some of its initiative at critical moments.

Real Cities, InfiNet and other NCN spin-offs

Real Media, Inc., yet another, more independent effort, operated as a close friend and/or rival to the NCN, despite claims to the contrary.[26] When Knight Ridder launched its Real Cities network for ads as an outgrowth of its New Century Network, for example, in the fall of 1997, it involved 32 web sites run by newspapers. Robert Ingle, Knight Ridder Inc.'s New Media division president, said that his project was designed to become a national site network, like Microsoft's Sidewalk. Ingle added, somewhat prophetically, that the NCN was "still a notion with considerable power and potential but I do think the time window is getting shorter."[27]

Knight Ridder's InfiNet project, a division of Landmark Communications Inc., was invested in the creation and curation of web sites outside of New York City, including for such newspapers as the *Lexington Herald-Leader*. At $9.95 a month and 10 hours online, or $24.95 for up to 100 hours, it was an expensive proposition out of reach of most customers. Technically, Knight Ridder's effort was supposed to act in tandem with the larger NCN project. How that worked in reality was more than a little vague for these local and regional partners, however, including at suburban papers in New York state.[28] The Pottsville, Penn., *Republican* and *Evening Herald*, with a regional web site, called Schuykill OnLine, was another example of an InfiNet-affiliated site from this era. By April 1996, InfiNet had 45 affiliates, 28 of which were a part of Knight Ridder's contribution.[29] But from the beginning the company had grander plans.

In June 1995, Landmark and Knight Ridder owned about 35 daily newspapers, including major operations such as *Philadelphia Inquirer*, *Miami Herald*, *Detroit Free Press* and *San Jose Mercury News*, with the latter, and smaller, but still influential, newspapers, in the former case, like *The Virginian-Pilot*.[30]

The Knight Ridder and Landmark venture was imagined as a robust investment, a true competitor to Prodigy, with the idea that a user could turn on their computer and find what was essentially a web browser built for them. According to InfiNet's president, David D. Richards, the goal for the joint project was to create "an on-line network of 100 newspapers within" two years.[31] "InfiNet, being owned by two newspaper chains itself, expects to be able to more easily build trust with publishers . . . any InfiNet subscriber, accessing the Internet from a computer at home or work, will see the local newspaper's electronic greeting first." In other words, having a newspaper connection was thought of as a plus, not a liability.[32]

One industry analyst, Edward Atorino, believed that despite competition from established brands like *The New York Times* and *The Wall Street Journal*, InfiNet had the potential to act like a research and development operation, to test the viability of online news. "Whether or not it's a business or not, we'll know in the next five or so years. . . . But just in case, you've got to establish yourself to be in this business. You don't want to miss what could be your next big opportunity."[33] That just-in-case mentality was not uncommon in the mid-to-late 1990s with larger projects. With resources to spare, corporations like Knight Ridder, despite having had previously negative experiences, could still afford to try concepts out on a big scale.

InfiNet was built to prioritize content at the local level, including "pricing tiers," but the hope was that an independent subscriber base would make the service more self-reliant, with a larger proportion of online content free. But again, how a company could provide hard-to-develop journalism for free while also encouraging readers to pay at least something was unclear. InfiNet was intended as a kind of support system for this, to be fair, providing "customer service, billing, market research and other services. It will actually operate the network and provide the links that will give the newspapers' electronic subscribers access to the internet." Any resulting revenues (primarily from some specialized advertising, subscriber fees or both) would be shared.[34]

However unrealistic from the perspective of the present, it is important to take some of these aspirations at some sort of face value. Both the NCN and its quasi-rivals like InfiNet did not have much in the way of role models for what they were doing or hoped to do. Even cable and satellite TV were conceptualized around a different kind of product—live content—and not on the mixture of static text and images, and some early audio and video, that was the early internet. In the meantime, the NCN was supposed to be acting as a kind of umbrella for these and other efforts—an ad for the NCN on its first-year anniversary proclaimed.

> *We are acutely aware that powerful Internet competition is fast approaching each of us. We believe that working together is one way to secure a solid share of online subscribers in each of our markets. We recognize most of all that success depends on accepting that the Internet is a legitimate new medium, to which our customers are responding with fervor.*[35]

Running in *Editor & Publisher*, it is an example of how confident the NCN partners—at least publicly—were in the early stages of their endeavor. And yet, while this study is not a business history, per se, or an analysis of the early online marketplace, the uncoordinated, ill-defined mission of the NCN *was* effective at countering other, large corporate efforts such as those led by Microsoft, but not as effective at fighting off young start-ups, especially the nimble Craigslist, which operating less like a tech giant (like the perennial villain, Microsoft) and more like a guerilla force, meeting customer needs while remaining light on the ground and living off the land.[36]

Microsoft as the original evil empire

A critical consideration in all of this is the fear of Microsoft, and to a lesser degree, Apple and Yahoo!—not yet Amazon and Google, per se. Google was considered a tentative ally of newspapers, while Amazon was still not the all-encompassing behemoth it would later become (and its CEO, Jeff Bezos, was years away from becoming a beneficent publisher in the old style).

Indeed, the launch of Microsoft's various quasi-journalistic efforts (including the Microsoft Network) is arguably one of the main reasons the NCN was initiated—it is important to remember how the NCN was in many ways a reaction, and not a proactively formed coalition of the willing.[37]

"Do you think Microsoft will hesitate to grab your share of the online take? Then why should newspapers sit and wait? All of the old reasons for newspapers to hesitate have vanished into the cyber-thin air of the Web/ Mosaic world."[38]

Editor & Publisher technology columnist Michael Conniff's rhetorical question and main point in early 1995 was shared by many others.[39] A special fear was tied to how Microsoft had a nearly unrivaled ability to bundle software with hardware, and thus had the power to push readers away from nascent news sites or collaborations with companies more open to making deals with publishers, such as Netscape or America Online.[40] In an era when access to email was not free, this concern was legitimate.[41] Microsoft's Internet Explorer 3, launched in August 1996, may have been exciting for tech-industry watchers, but not for newspaper companies, who worried about the browser's claim to offer "free access (connect charges may apply) to popular content such as that from ESPNET SportsZone and The Wall Street Journal Interactive Edition, and exclusive access to content on sites such as Hollywood Online."[42]

Newsroom leaders writing letters to *Editor & Publisher* tried to put on a brave face. Peter Levitan, president of New Jersey Online and Journal Square Interactive, said that as of October 1996, some 200 newspapers had online sites that covered their local communities well. "There is a reason that newspapers continue to lead all other media in ad revenue. We deliver relevance from our home bases. Not from Redmond, Wash." [Washington state, USA, where Microsoft was headquartered].[43] Others were more circumspect, especially since *The Wall Street Journal* had agreed to partner with the tech company with its early, paywalled site.

The paper's valuation was $2.2 billion in November 2016, thanks in no small part to the partnership with Microsoft, which brought in 100,000 subscribers (at this point, outside of those connected to Microsoft, the site had an additional 30,000 subscribers). Another part of the paper's initial online success was its hyper-focus on financial news. Contemporaries thought its example might be tough to emulate because of the "business publishing," "financial information" corporate-market-driven nature of its news coverage. It was almost what a later generation of online-news pioneers would call a "vertical," or single-issue site.[44]

"The interactive edition is definitely driven out of a traditional newspaper model with advertising picking up the bigger share of the freight," noted Josephine Ottman, the product marketing director for Dow Jones, which owned the paper. The browsing model of the traditional newspaper was still thought to be effective, in the midst of this; Ottman noted that the online version of the paper, "allows people to act on their interests as they discover them."[45]

In addition to its high-profile partnerships (not just with *The Wall Street Journal*, but also in the form of its own magazine, *Slate*, launched in 1996), Microsoft's threat was embodied in its Sidewalk program, which was an attempt to create local city arts and entertainment guides, the kind of content that large American daily newspapers used to attract marque advertisers, which concerned even larger chains such as Knight Ridder, which tried to create their own online alternative sites in response.[46] Other concerns centered around a supposed theft of editorial talent by Microsoft, which could pay far more than even a nationally respected paper like the *Chicago Tribune*.[47]

Microsoft was thus a multilayered threat, with an online presence, and the capacity to expand into new areas quickly and in force, including early online TV projects (its WebTV Networks).[48] Into 1997, and the (brief) heyday of the NCN, newspaper owners, editors and their staffs, along with their allies in the technology industry that were not Microsoft, seemed to operate in a kind of worst-case presumptive state about the company, with one fretting that it "has supposedly set aside several million dollars to develop local content." Another worried that it "is integrating in its assault on the local classified market."[49]

Even seasoned industry veterans who had made the difficult jump to successfully running newspaper sites were concerned. Candy Thompson, who was the sales director for online directories at Digital Ink Co., which was, in turn, owned by the *Washington Post*, argued newspapers had "to be willing to put in more financially," be more flexible about pricing online ads and be more aggressive about seeking out new markets and partners.[50] Other contemporaries agreed: risk, and not caution, was key to experimenting with the kinds of specialized ads that technology firms like Microsoft and Yahoo! were going after, including those for cars and jobs.[51]

And while Microsoft officially downplayed its role as online-ad usurper, and even went so far as to sponsor a summer 1997 Newspaper Association of America (NAA) conference focused on online news, prominent newspaper industry leaders remained chilly, or even hostile.[52]

Knight Ridder's president of new media, Bob Ingle, declared in a well-covered keynote address that "you dance with the devil and you pay the price," referring to Microsoft as an existential threat, claiming that its CEO at the time, Bill Gates, was aiming for the newspaper industry's ad *and* content elements, "spending between $400 million and $600 million a year on content. . . . I doubt if the entire newspaper industry is spending as much as $400 million a year on all its new media efforts. So what does Microsoft see that the newspapers seem unable to see?"[53] While there are some exceptions, he said that "far too many [newspapers] have done little or nothing to create interactive entertainment guides and other directories to gain competitive advantage over Sidewalk, Digital City and others seeking to crack this lucrative local online market."[54]

Outside of incendiary speeches, the tensions between Microsoft and the journalism industry played out in the pages of the latter's trade publications. There were lingering concerns about how the former's web-filtering software would impact news sites.[55] There were smaller snubs, too, like how *The Seattle Times* went with Sun Microsystems and Netscape for its web-publishing software, server operating system and networking software, instead of Microsoft.[56] The company fought back, hiring a lobbying firm in Washington, DC, and contesting antitrust legal actions from the federal government.[57]

Later, after the demise of the NCN, the tenor of coverage of Microsoft seemed to change, especially after the latter developed MSNBC in partnership with NBC News.[58] And despite the Sidewalk project's size—with some 300 employees, the national network of entertainment guides had about $26 million in ads sold to 6,000 advertisers in 1998—it was considered, in the end, less of a threat than perhaps warranted. Anxiety shifted to the fate of paid online advertising and then the impact of the 1999–2000 tech bubble's epic bursting.[59] Even profiles of *Slate* (along with *Salon*) became more favorable.[60] That is not to say that Microsoft became a beloved partner of newspapers—far from it—but other tech companies were eventually seen as actual, and not just perceived, threats, especially as search engines improved in the 2000s.[61]

As one 2007 retrospective put it, "An eternity ago in the Internet era, in 1997, Microsoft tried to launch its own version of a digital daily, called *Sidewalk*. Newspapers, sensing the threat, declined to cooperate with it, and *Sidewalk* bombed."[62] That story was, of course, more complex, for the reasons outlined earlier. But in the midst of *Sidewalk's* retreat, the NCN left the scene, replaced by a multiplicity of separate efforts—with the industry deciding to abandon a collective response to the internet, and with each individual company going their own way.

The NCN's collapse and what it meant

Despite a late pivot to become a more formal ad network in mid-1997, and then a still-later bid in late 1997 to become a kind of search engine, the NCN shut down after three years in March 1998. As *Editor & Publisher*'s Steve Outing observed, the effort "was beset by a lack of consensus among its owners about what online businesses it should be engaged in." A particular weakness was the forced consensus that the NCN operated under, he noted, with a charter requiring "that at least a strong majority of the founders agree on any particular NCN business venture . . . insider reports indicate that that sort of consensus was difficult to achieve."[63]

As has been explored earlier, Knight Ridder had its own, competing ventures. But in this just-in-case parallel effort, it had been joined by Cox and Tribune Co.—hardly the stuff of a confident, united front. While Real Media took over some of what remained, it was considered a near-total dead end at the time.[64]

Despite the lack of focus and the competing projects by its founding companies, the NCN *could* have conceivably found a path forward in its original, ambitious effort to coordinate online ads on its various members' newspaper sites. A longer analysis showed that the NCN had, in fact, planned to launch its own search engine and directory service plan, codenamed, "On Ramp," which had an interesting premise but not enough time to continue past the conceptual-planning stages.[65]

According to this account, one possibility would have been the outright purchase of a search engine, and failing to do so may have been a "major strategic mistake, according to a growing number of internet media authorities."[66] The fear was that by the time newspapers *did* think of an alternative to the NCN, it would be too late, with new and established search engines (and there were number of competitors at this point, from Yahoo! to Excite, with Google becoming a dominating force later on).[67]

The brief life of the On Ramp project (from August 1997 onward) had itself been a kind of compromise—true to the NCN's nature, it was *not* a consensus decision. The idea would have been to pursue a willing search-engine company that would have partnered with the NCN's affiliate newspaper sites, "to co-brand its pages with news sites in exchange for new ad revenues (or perhaps licensing fees) from the newspapers . . . the kind of pages that you see when you visit a site like Yahoo! or Infoseek would reside on a newspaper's Web site." At a November 1997 meeting, the idea of buying their own search engine was mentioned with enthusiasm—but at that late hour.[68]

The NCN and other media companies' own analysis had already concluded that newspaper sites were "getting killed by Yahoo!, et al." While local advertising was important online, national web advertising had remained elusive for newspapers. Classified ads were threatened too. Finding a way to profitability for news sites was not just optional—it was necessary, and that was becoming clearer by the month.[69] While the NCN On Ramp project had succeeded in constructing "an elaborate prototype" of how a web-searchable coalition of news sites could work, even if they had, it would have been ahead of its time.[70]

At least one NCN executive, Stacey Artandi, who had been the vice president of business development for NCN, had been a supporter of an aggressive online ad network, including finding a more direct partner to work with, in the form of a friendly search engine.[71] To some extent, that would happen, though in a more roundabout way, with Google's AdSense program. How that development would impact newsroom practices, along with the more widespread adoption of original online news, will be explored in the next couple of chapters.

In any event, the NCN's final collapse was not necessarily preordained. More friendly online-ad companies like Classifieds2000 *could* have helped onramp the NCN into a more viable operation.[72] But the NCN's demise happened within the larger context of the foggy future of online news. Other possibilities were still there, for "umbrella organizations" within the newspaper industry, such as Zip2, which specialized in online ads for newspaper sites, and other, "individual newspaper companies—including the *Boston Globe*, Times Mirror and Hollinger/ Southam Newspapers in Canada . . . pursuing search/directory deals on their own or in concert with other newspapers," were prepared to go it alone.[73]

Out of the ashes of the NCN emerged Classified Ventures, which started as a collaboration by the Tribune Co., Times Mirror Co. and Washington Post Co. In addition, Knight Ridder and Gannett affiliated with the effort, with a combined 147 newspapers, in 42 states, or 35 of the country's top 50 media markets. A parallel effort by the Newspaper Association of America was trying to connect 40 newspapers and trying to get online ads more searchable.[74] A decade later, in an echo of this effort, the Associated Press' Mobile News Network signed on 107 papers, from the *San Jose Mercury News* to the *Billings Gazette* (Montana) to the *Herald & Review* (Illinois). It was designed for early smartphones.[75]

Conclusion

The NCN was not meant to be an all-encompassing response to the internet—it was not a holistic program—but it was a rare example of cooperation for the major players in an industry notorious for solo thinking. While some contemporaries dismissed it, perhaps rightly, as a demonstrative experiment meant to reassure nervous shareholders, smart people believed in the effort enough to dedicate prime parts of their early careers to it. It would be unfair to write the NCN and similar projects off as mere show efforts. Instead, it is important to consider them on their own, if contextualized merits, not as doomed, but as aspirational, complex and perhaps too soon.

The fate of the NCN and similar efforts reflects just how murky the future was in the mid-to-late 1990s with the internet. The NCN's original goal had been to share software development, links, advertising networks and, most critically, the lucrative classified advertising market, which composed some 38 percent of the newspaper industry's total advertising budget in 1997, or about 40 percent in 1998, worth about $18 billion.[76] While this loose confederation of sites was disbanded by the spring of 1998, it ultimately represented an effort to improve nearly 150 newspaper sites in 42 states, and 35 of the country's top 50 markets.[77]

The failure of the NCN to escape the corporate gravity of its collective, and sometimes at cross-purposes, parents, shows how seriously both major and minor players took the creation of standardized site interfaces, online classified ad search capacities, and the overall user experience. As the *Editor & Publisher* editorial board put it, "For far too long into the interactive era, the newspaper industry's grasp of the threat the internet posed to its classified advertising franchise reminded us of Mark Twain's famous line about the weather: Everybody talks about it, but nobody ever does anything about it. . . . In the truly brand-new online environment, there were no models for success. Simply put, the newspaper industry—and all its would-be competitors—had not failed enough yet."[78]

While a brave face, this statement belied the reality that there was *not* a lot more time left, at least not a lot left for the industry to truly fail without serious repercussions.

While this study hopes to push back against the idea that major news-media companies brought calamity on themselves, the NCN is a kind of extended example of what could and did go wrong. And yet, again, it made sense for its moment. As Elliott King pointed out in his 2010 book on the ways that journalism was being transformed by the internet, online service providers like AOL had made sweeping deals with Knight Ridder and the Tribune Company, and Cox Newspapers and Times Mirror were cooperating with Prodigy. The idea was that established tech companies would provide the technical know-how and that the newspapers, and media corporations who owned them, would be the brand-name information—i.e., news—providers. CNN was doing something similar, via CNN On-line, with help from CompuServe.[79]

And for a while, that idea made a lot of innate sense, both on the ground with the rank-and-file news workers who applied the internet to their journalistic labor, and to their editors, publishers and owners. In time, of course, as we know, looking back, that would change, and change quickly.

The next chapter explores how the first generation of news workers used the internet in their daily working lives, including how they interacted with those now-ubiquitous tools called search engines.

Notes

1 Steve Outing, "NCN Goes Belly Up—Total Shutdown Announced: Three Years and $9 Million After Nine Newspaper Companies Attempted to Create a Consortium to Dominate the Internet News Business, They've Given Up," *Editor & Publisher*, March 14, 1998, 12, 14. For an excellent standalone study on the history of the NCN, see John C. Speer, "The New Century Network: A Critical Moment for Newspapers at the Dawn of the Internet" (MA thesis, University of Maryland, 2013).

2 John Consoli, "Online Timetable: New Century Network Hopes to Have Its National Network of Local Online Services Operational Within Two Years," *Editor & Publisher*, July 1, 1995, 17; Steve Outing, "NCN Goes Belly Up—Total Shutdown Announced: Three Years and $9 Million After Nine Newspaper Companies Attempted to Create a Consortium to Dominate the Internet News Business, They've Given Up," *Editor & Publisher*, March 14, 1998, 12, 14.

3 "NCN Alliance," *Editor & Publisher*, May 6, 1995, 6.

4 Infinet and other efforts will be discussed more below, while Nando.net will be discussed in a later chapter; see Katherine Fulton, "www.journalism.now: A Tour of Our Uncertain Future," *Columbia Journalism Review*, March–April 1996, 19–26; Fulton discussed the New Century Network and its peers on p. 25, including the tantalizing idea of micro-payments for journalism, before that idea took off in more detail: "One longed-for innovation so far remains elusive—that secure transactions on-line will yield whole new profit lines (calendar listings tied to ticket sales, for instance). And what about citizens and consumers?" Fulton was a former Nieman Fellow and a technology consultant who had started her own alt-weekly in North Carolina, the *Independent*, and done some college teaching.

5 Christine Ogan and Randy Beam, "Internet Challenges for Media Businesses," in *The Internet and American Business*, eds. William Aspray and Paul Ceruzzi (Cambridge, MA: MIT Press, 2008), 279–314; see also Atsushi Akera, "Communities and Specialized Information Businesses," in *The Internet and American Business*, eds. William Aspray and Paul Ceruzzi (Cambridge, MA: MIT Press, 2008), 423–47.

6 Jessa Lingel, *An Internet for the People: The Politics and Promise of Craigslist* (Princeton, NJ: Princeton University Press, 2020); she cites, in turn, the work of Clayton M. Christensen, Michael E. Raynor and Rory McDonald; see "What Is Disruptive Innovation? Twenty Years After the Introduction of the Theory, We Revisit What It Does—and Doesn't—Explain," *Harvard Business Review*, December 2015, https://hbr.org/2015/12/what-is-disruptive-innovation.

7 Lingel, *An Internet for the People*, 46.

8 Ibid., 47.

9 Ibid., 47.

10 Ibid., 47–48. See also "A quick history of Cox Automotive," www.coxautoinc.com/about-us/our-history/.

11 Lucia Moses, "Classified Struggle: Battling the Monster, and Other Tales from the Online Front Lines," *Editor & Publisher*, September 18, 2000, 6–8, 10; see also "About Us," https://hiring.careerbuilder.com/company/about-us; "About Monster," www.monster.com/about/.

12 Pablo Boczkowski, *Digitizing the News: Innovation in Online Newspapers* (Cambridge, MA: MIT Press, 2005), 59.

13 A few of these innovations will be showcased in this chapter, but others will follow, building on the work of Pablo Boczkowski and Megan Sapner Ankerson, among others. For more specifically on how these played out in early online newsrooms/newsrooms that were early to get online, see the next chapter.
14 Lingel, *An Internet for the People*, 48–49.
15 For more on mythmaking in journalism, see Jack Lule, *Daily News, Eternal Stories: The Mythological Role of Journalism* (New York: The Guilford Press, 2001).
16 Hoag Levins, "In Search of: Internet Busine$$ [sic]: Will Web Publishing Mature from a Media Fad to a Profitable Enterprise," *Editor & Publisher*, February 8, 1997, 4–6.
17 Ibid.
18 David Noack, "Off Line Newspapers: Too Busy, Too Small, or Too Unsure, Some More Slowly into Cyberspace," *Editor & Publisher*, February 8, 1997, 32–33, 40.
19 Ken Liebeskind, "The Battle for Help Wanted: Newspapers Defend the Franchise by Going on the Offensive and Taking the War for Help-Wanted Ads to the Contenders' Turf," *Editor & Publisher*, February 8, 1997, 8, 10.
20 B. G. Yovich, "Meeting the Online Competition: Guiding Principles from an Online Newspaper Veteran and an Educator: Make Friends, Move Fast, Scan the Horizon," *Editor & Publisher*, February 8, 1997, 18–19, 23.
21 Mark Fitzgerald, "Newspapers Go It Alone into Cyberspace," *Editor & Publisher*, February 22, 1997, 7, 42.
22 Ibid., 7, 42.
23 Hoag Levins, "First Aggregated Newspaper Web Site," *Editor & Publisher*, April 26, 1997, 84–85.
24 Anonymous staff writer, "In short," *Editor & Publisher*, July 26, 1997, 26.
25 This comment from Jerry Ceppos, of Knight Ridder, is illuminating: "There is a chance that the cartoonist was trying for irony, but I think not. He . . . merely reflected the prevailing view inside the newsroom. Thus, all of those folks have ownership of the collapse of newsrooms;" personal correspondence with author, February 14, 2021.
26 Hoag Levins, "NCN and Real Media Bury the Hatchet: Former Market Foes Announce Partnership That Includes Coordinated Online Ad Sales Campaigns," *Editor & Publisher*, December 13, 1997, 46–47.
27 Steve Outing, "K-R Launches 'Real Cities' Ad Network: Placement on 32 Web Sites," *Editor & Publisher*, October 25, 1997, 47.
28 "Knight-Ridder Ky. Papers Starts Kentucky Connect," "Online Liability Decision Stands," "N.Y. Times Stays on AOL," "On the Web in N.Y. Suburbs," "Anderson Takes Indiana Online," *Editor & Publisher*, January 13, 1996, 28–29.
29 "Pennsy Paper Joins InfiNet," *Editor & Publisher*, January 13, 1996, 35.
30 "Knight-Ridder Buys into InfiNet[:] An On-line Network of 100 Papers Is Planned," *The Virginian-Pilot*, June 8, 1995, 1, accessed September 2, 2021, https://scholar.lib.vt.edu/VA-news/VA-Pilot/issues/1995/vp950608/06080415.htm.
31 Ibid.
32 Ibid.
33 Ibid.
34 Ibid.

35 "United We Stand," *Editor & Publisher*, April 13, 1996, 43.
36 For yet another example of how this played out in the web's early development—this process of niche companies (sometimes, for there were many flare-outs and dead-ends) succeeding in fulfilling niche needs, see Christine Lagorio-Chafkin, *We Are the Nerds: The Birth and Tumultuous Life of Reddit, the Internet's Culture Laboratory* (New York: Hachette Books, 2018); Brian McCullough, *How the Internet Happened: From Netscape to the iPhone* (New York: W.W. Norton, 2018); the ways that both Lagorio-Chafkin and McCullough focus on the impact of particular personalities on the history of the web, as well as the critical nature of the years from about 1993 through 2008, which this book also focuses on.
37 David M. Cole and Christopher J. Feola, "Paper Partners: Former Rivals Join Hands to Face Uncertain Future," *Quill*, September 1995, 31–33; Anonymous Staff Writer, "Editor & Publisher Launches on the World Wide Web," *Editor & Publisher*, June 24, 1995, 68.
38 Michael Conniff, "A Tangled Web for Newspapers," *Editor & Publisher*, February 4, 1995, 25.
39 Jodi B. Cohen, "Browsers and Newspapers," *Editor & Publisher*, September 21, 1996, 30.
40 Ibid; see also Christopher J. Feola and James Brown, "Gates Hatches MSN: Microsoft Ventures into Digital News Delivery," *Quill*, September 1995, 34–36.
41 Cohen, "Browsers and Newspapers," 30.
42 Anonymous Staff Writer, "Microsoft Launches Microsoft Internet Explorer 3.0 with Exclusive, Free Content Offers from Top Web Sites," *Microsoft PressPass*, August 16, 1995, accessed September 3, 2021, https://news.microsoft.com/1996/08/13/microsoft-launches-microsoft-internet-explorer-3-0-with-exclusive-free-content-offers-from-top-web-sites/.
43 Peter Levitan, "Who's Afraid of Microsoft?" *Editor & Publisher*, October 12, 1996, 7.
44 Jodi B. Cohen, "Online Early and Still Going," *Editor & Publisher*, November 16, 1996, 26–27.
45 Ibid; Ottman again:
"People tend to think of us at the newspaper, and then they think we have these ancillary businesses. But we were online before online was cool," 26.
46 Note that at various points "Knight Ridder" was hyphenated, but to be consistent this author usually used the non-hyphenated version, as this seems most prevalent in the trade literature. Steve Outing, "Knight-Ridder Counterattacks 'Sidewalk'," *Editor & Publisher*, May 10, 1997, 28, 33; Steve Outing, "City-Search Signs Washington Post," *Editor & Publisher*, June 14, 1997, 36; "About Us," *Slate*, accessed September 3, 2021, https://slate.com/about.
47 Mark Fitzgerald, "Sidewalk's Side: Execs for Microsoft's Online City Guides Say That Despite the Wording of Their Recruitment Ads, They Are Looking for New Media People, not 'Editorial People'," *Editor & Publisher*, June 14, 1997, 9–10.
48 Michael J. Bugeja and Kandice Salomone, "Sounding the Alarm on PV TVs," *Editor & Publisher*, July 12, 1997, 48, 29.
49 Dori Perrucci, "Experimenting with Online Classifieds: Newspapers Discuss Their Approaches During NAA Conference," *Editor & Publisher*, July 26, 1997, 18.
50 Ibid.

51 Perrucci, "Experimenting with Online Classifieds," 16–18; Hoag Levins, "Papers Strike Back at Microsoft's Classifies: In a Direct Assault on Microsoft CarPoint, Three of the Nation's Largest Newspaper Companies Pool Their Resources to Create Cars.com," *Editor & Publisher*, December 27, 1997, 20, 21.

52 Hoag Levins, "Knight-Ridder Exec Blasts Bill Gates: Connections' 97 Keynote Speaker Roger Ingle Sounds an Industry Call to Arms Against Microsoft," *Editor & Publisher*, July 26, 1997, 24–25.

53 Ibid; in a previous confrontation, at a conference in Chicago, Ingle had denounced Gates minutes after the latter spoke, during a Q&A, accusing him of stealing news workers for Microsoft. According to the *Editor & Publisher* account: "Ingle also asked Gates why newspapers should purchase software products from a company that is using its profits to fund new kinds of online competition against newspapers."; Todd Haselton and Jordan Novet, "Bill Gates Leaves Microsoft Board," *CNBC*, March 13, 2020, accessed September 3, 2021, www.cnbc.com/2020/03/13/bill-gates-leaves-microsoft-board.html.

54 Levins, "Knight-Ridder Exec Blasts Bill Gates," 24–25.

55 David Noack, "Ratings Proposed for Web Sites: Microsoft and Sony Among Those Crafting New Rules for 'Rating' Online Journalism," *Editor & Publisher*, August 23, 1997, 11–12.

56 David Noack, "*Seattle Times* Shuns Microsoft Software: Nasty Words Between Two Internet Publishers Competing for the Same Online Readers and Advertisings in the Pacific Northwest," *Editor& Publisher*, September 27, 1997, 30–31.

57 "Microsoft's Lobbying Offensive: Washington Onslaught Planned," *Editor & Publisher*, December 27, 1997, 20, 21.

58 Mark Fitzgerald, "Defending Web Journalism: Merrill Brown Speaks Out on Journalism Standards, Audience Measurement," *Editor & Publisher*, February 14, 1998, 50; Brian Stelter, "MSNBC.com May Change Its Name," *The New York Times*, October 6, 2010, accessed September 3, 2021, www.nytimes.com/2010/10/07/business/media/07msnbc.html.

59 Martha L. Stone, "Microsoft Re-lays Sidewalk: But Analysts Doubt New Site Will Threaten Newspapers or Their City Guides," *Editor & Publisher*, October 24, 1998, 28.

60 Martha L. Stone, "A Clean Slate for Microsoft: Microsoft's Webzine Is Free Again—Promoting Itself and Updating Its Image," *Editor & Publisher*, April 3, 1999, 30; Christopher J. Feola, "Beware, the Great Satan: Is It Bill Gates and Michael Kinsley or the Folks 'Writing' for the Digerati?" *Quill*, September 1996, 12–13; Nicholas Stein, "Slate vs. Salon: The Leading Online Magazines Struggle to Get the Net," *Columbia Journalism Review*, January–February 1999, 56–59.

61 Mark Fitzgerald and Jennifer Saba, "Is Yahoo the Right Fit? Newspapers Partnered with Online Ad Giant—Now Microsoft Wants It—but Other Options Remain," *Editor & Publisher*, March 2008, 42–44, 46.

62 Steve Outing, "NCN Goes Belly Up—Total Shutdown Announced: Three Years and $9 Million After Nine Newspaper Companies Attempted to Create a Consortium to Dominate the Internet News Business, They've Given Up," *Editor & Publisher*, March 14, 1998, 12.

63 Ibid., 14.

64 Ibid.

65 Steve Outing, "Online Newspapers' Biggest Mistake? Did the Industry's Failure to Recognize the Crucial Importance of National Search Engine Capacity Doom It to Second Place or Worse?" *Editor & Publisher*, March 14, 1998, 42, 44–45.
66 Ibid.
67 Ibid.
68 Ibid.
69 Ibid., 43.
70 Ibid.
71 The NCN focused its work *just* on online ads in its last month or so, before it closed completely, but this seems to have been an exceptionally brief episode, more of a final bit of transition before it was formally shut down than a serious effort; see Outing, "Online Newspapers' Biggest Mistake?" 44.
72 "Reports from others close to the On Ramp project indicate that during the last two months before it closed, NCN had been talking about breaking off part of itself into a separate entity. The proposal apparently would have taken the search engine component of NCN and spun it off to an affiliated company or subsidiary—one which not all of NCN's nine media company owners would be part of, but presumably only those that agreed with the strategy and that do not have investments that would run counter to it. (The Tribune Co., one of NCN's nine founding companies, owns a chunk of Excite, which might logically position it to avoid a search/directory' newspaper deal with one of Excite's competitors, for instance.)" See Outing, "Online Newspapers' Biggest Mistake?" 45.
73 Outing, "Online Newspapers' Biggest Mistake?" 45.
74 Anonymous Staff Writer, "Position Wanted: Newspaper Dominance of Online Classifieds," *Editor & Publisher*, June 13, 1998, 4.
75 Jennifer Saba, "When You Duck Inside with Mobile: You've Gotta Lotta Verve," *Editor & Publisher*, June 2008, 8, 9.
76 Jeff VonKaenel, "Will the Big Dailies Be Extinct in 10 Years?" *Editor & Publisher*, January 11, 1997, 56; Martha L. Stone, "Papers Face Serious Classified Threats: While Kicking Off a Major Initiative to Help Newspapers Fight Back, API's Conference Highlights Major Threats to Classified Advertising for the Next Century," *Editor & Publisher*, August 1, 1998, 26–27.
77 "In Review: And Now, Today's Earthquake News: Yahoo! San Francisco: www.sfbay.yahoo.com," *Editor & Publisher*, July 26, 1997, 26; Outing, "Online Newspapers' Biggest Mistake?" 42, 44–45; Anonymous Staff Writer, "Position Wanted," 4.
78 Anonymous Staff Writer, "Position Wanted," 4.
79 Elliott King, *Free for All: The Internet's Transformation of Journalism* (Evanston, IL: Northwestern University Press, 2010). See also Dan Gillmor, *We the Media: Grassroots Journalism by the People, for the People* (Sebastopol, CA: O'Reilly, 2004); John Pavlik, *Journalism and New Media* (New York: Columbia University Press, 2001); Philip Meyer, *The Vanishing Newspaper: Saving Journalism in the Information Age*. 2nd ed. (Columbia, MO: University of Missouri, 2009).

4 The internet and newsgathering in the late 1990s and early 2000s

When journalists used the internet in the late 1990s and early 2000s, how did they use it, and why did they use it? And how similar (or not) was it to the computer-assisted reporting (CAR) movement of that same era? This chapter and the next explore these questions, focusing on rank-and-file news workers in their newsroom contexts, and looking at how the internet impacted day-to-day work practices. It moves away from some of the higher level discussions in the previous two chapters.

As with any new technology or set of technologies, the use of the internet in newsrooms by journalists was gradual, and not a sudden phenomenon, though in retrospect it certainly feels sudden. This is evident from a close reading of dozens of journalism textbooks from the era, as well as memoirs, trade publications and industry reports. And while theories of technology diffusion, adoption and disruption provide helpful interpretations as to why things happened the way that they did, they do not always provide concrete examples of these processes in action.[1]

Much like the earlier adoptions of electric typewriters, terminals and, eventually, desktop computers and early laptops, along with datatransmission tools, the use of the internet for searching for expert sources, previous stories and other facts happened slowly, then seemingly all at once. Pablo Boczkowski talks about how the first generation of online newsrooms engaged in a cautious process of "hedging," a concept he defines as a conservative attempt to move in many, sometimes counterbalancing, directions, in response to market uncertainties and the accompanying risk of sunk financial investments.[2] This was after a period of "settling"—the closure or coalescing around the idea of independent or at most loosely affiliated web sites, not online services such as CompuServe, AOL or Prodigy—as being the best way forward in the face of that uncertainty.[3]

Rather than acting out of fear, as Boczkowski points out, newspapers built news sites and encouraged their reporting staffs to work for them (to varying degrees), as part of a kind of creative conservativism, with most news

DOI: 10.4324/9780429324871-4

organizations "usually more interested in finding out what the new technologies meant for the print enterprise than in more offensively developing new technical, communication and organization capabilities." That meant that "American dailies . . . ran behind the development of the web, following the lead of early entrants such as Netscape and Yahoo, even though they had been experimenting with online environments before these companies were formed." Conversely, that *also* meant that when newspapers and their staffs *did* eventually act, they could be quite capable, repurposing, recreating, or recombining content in interesting and innovative ways (putting print stories on their sites, customizing their content or going deeper into topics, and emphasizing "live" content, or creating special, original content just for their sites, respectively).[4]

How that worked in practice involved the careful preservation of newsroom practices, with a few new ones, including how news workers in these spaces went about their daily journalistic tasks. Having made the push to move (generally) toward the internet as a *complementary* (not yet a *replacement*) medium, most newsrooms preserved practices that had been helpful before, while in some limited cases trying out new approaches to their work.[5]

Boczkowski believed that contrary to some interpretations of the newspaper industry as overly cautious, worried about pouring too much money and personnel into web-based operations in the late 1990s after the expensive Viewtron project (for Knight Ridder) and videotex more broadly, a perspective advocated for by scholars such as John Pavlik, that caution was giving way to initiative by the end of the 1990s.[6]

The newsroom when the civilian internet was still new: the mid-to-late 1990s

In many ways, how reporters and editors thought of the use of the internet for reporting was framed by the ongoing incorporation of CAR techniques. The origin of that movement, with its use of software to construct and interpret databases, but also, later, to use search-engine tools, geolocation data, and other digital approaches to telling complex stories, is explored by C.W. Anderson.[7] While it is beyond the scope of this study to outline that history, it is important to remember that by the mid-1990s, CAR advocates such as Nora Paul, Brant Houston, Bruce Garrison and Kathleen Wickham, among others, were early adopters of, and enthusiasts for, the use of the new commercial internet for journalistic research and writing.

They followed, loosely, the example of Philip Meyer, whose *Precision Journalism* text, published in 1973, called for a more social-scientific approach to journalism as opposed to a literary or impressionistic one.[8] In practice, CAR, sometimes referred to as computer-assisted journalism or computer-assisted investigative reporting (CAIR), with the latter described by Margaret DeFleur, evolved into a more pragmatic, tool-based way of doing journalism, as opposed to a philosophy regarding the use of data.[9]

For many journalists, the use of the internet for their work was at first a rare occurrence, despite a (gradually) growing online readership. However, by the middle of 1999, 106 million people, or about 40 percent of all Americans, were online, with web advertising growing from $267 million in 1996 to $3 billion in 2003.[10] Reporters and their editors were increasingly exposed to the internet and its affordances at home, much as they had been during the 1980s, with personal computing. That meant that CAR approaches to their work became less alien over time, and more part of mainstream discourse in the publications such as *Editor & Publisher*, *Quill*, *Columbia Journalism Review* and the *Press Gazette*.[11]

Still, a certain reticence marked the use of the internet as a reporting tool, and CAR more generally. Shawn McIntosh, a reporter who specialized in CAR and who had left *USA Today* to work with the metro desk at *The Dallas Morning News*, warned his peers in a fall 1993 guide in *Quill* that the use of a computer for reporting allowed one to "answer questions that couldn't otherwise be answered and find stories that might otherwise remain hidden," calling CAR a "powerful tool, but one that is rarely painless, seldom cheap, and never easy to use. Don't be fooled by the media hype when you decide to make the big jump in your newsroom."[12] With CAR applications and the internet, some reporters were first exposed to its potential via listservs, and before that, Newsnet newsgroups.[13]

Listservs

Throughout the 1990s, SPJ-L, IRE-L, CARR-L, NICAR-L and FOI-L (for the Society of Professional Journalists, Investigative Reporters and Editors, National Institute for Computer-Assisted Reporting, and the Freedom of Information Act, respectively), essentially freewheeling email listservs with varying degrees of moderation, helped to facilitate discussions and resource-sharing among news workers who were online early, and then often.[14] Sometimes these conversations went a bit off the rails. Michael Ravnitzky, a law student who was active on some of them, thought they sometimes felt "like a newspaper without an editor," due to the hands-off nature of their moderation, which could lead to them being taken over by arguments or conspiracies, at least briefly, but some were better than others at controlling that kind of spiral.[15]

CARR-L in particular, though, was a favorite for those brave enough to log in, either from home or in some cases, via limited access in the newsroom, in the first few years of the 1990s. Among other topics, it covered how-to guides and training for CAR techniques, job postings, and how to get email access to the White House. According to one estimate, electronic journals and newsletters grew from 110 in 1991 to 240 in 1993, with discussion lists growing from 517 to 1,152 during that time.[16] Savvy news workers would still check out new postings on various sub-newsgroups on Usenet, which in 1993 still numbered well over 4,000 strong, but also specialized lists, such as "ProfNet," i.e., the "Professors Network," started in fall 1992 by Dan Forbush and designed to be a clearinghouse for sources for journalists interested in talking to experts. The service fielded requests by reporters to 540 public-information officers at 240 universities and colleges, labs, and government institutions, with responses by email, fax, phone or mail, whichever was preferred by the journalist.[17]

It is important to remember that the use of work email accounts, discussed more below, as part of online reporting, was a bit strange at first, for many reporters, who perhaps more used to forums and curated spaces such as Netscape and America Online, and so how-to guides for email-driven listservs served a key professionalization purpose. Email had been around since the Cold War, in various forms, but had been the domain of engineers and academics, not journalists. Listing one's email was a kind of sign of technological sophistication. Issues like the copyright status of email—especially if it was sent to a large number of people outside of one's newsroom—were still a bit unclear. But generally, the feeling among a number of news workers was that they needed to learn this new tool to be successful at their jobs. According to one expert, "[J]ournalism and [the] Internet have a mutual destiny that desperately needs to be explored. Professional journalists should be linking up to [the] Internet in droves."[18]

The internet was defined as a "network of networks' . . . [with] . . . 14,121 networks, 26,000 domains, 1.776 million host machines and an estimated 8 to 15 million individual users," part of the "toolbox of any computer-savvy, enterprising journalist." But beyond it being useful for research, "it's more: a community of professionals, acquaintances, colleagues, and friends; a treasure trove of developing and growing resources; an archive of facts and data; and an increasingly convenient way to retrieve beat-related information from AIDS research results through legal references to White House briefings."[19] Occasionally, this discourse surrounding the internet waxed poetic, with one SPJ writer declaring, "you soon realize that the only limit of the internet is your imagination."[20]

Databases and intranets

Perhaps more clear-eyed, or cynical, observers of the early internet's capacity as a research tool in the newsrooms of the mid-1990s saw that a key limitation was the number and kinds of records online—with governments at the national and state levels not always particularly keen or quick to digitize those records and make them readily available. Considerable attention was paid to this issue by the journalism industry's trade press throughout the decade.[21] Another concern included data storage, the hiring and retention of qualified personnel and training for those people—not every newspaper had an owner able and willing to spend $2 million on these areas, like Frank Daniels, Jr., the executive editor and owner of the *News & Observer* (and that was even before it was sold to McClatchy in August 1995 for $373 million). In that same year, many, even larger and well-funded newspapers, could not afford to put desktops at the workstation of every reporter in the newsroom, let alone connect them to the internet, and some debated the virtues of having a centralized database versus smaller, more distributed ones.[22]

The arrival of the internet went beyond simple searches, and this became clearer to newsroom leaders over time. The more sophisticated uses of the internet involved the creation of customized intranets—internally accessed internet portals. *The Seattle Times*, *Sacramento Bee*, *Atlanta Journal-Constitution*, *St. Petersburg Times*, the Raleigh *News & Observer* and the *Dayton* [Ohio] *Daily News* were among the first to build these for their news workers. There, reporters could access reporting resources, including specialized databases and directories, and early digitized archives, via these pages.[23] Internet-powered CAR tools included these portals, which allowed reporters to organize their notes and primary sources before uploading them to their content management systems (CMS).[24] CMS tools evolved during this era, moving from finicky, unfriendly interfaces to more useable ones.[25] Journalists were increasingly using more advanced, web-based tools, such as campaign-donor trackers.[26]

By 1998, the internet was becoming an increasingly common newsroom resource for "day-to-day reporting," as one survey of 45 newspapers in Texas showed.[27]

Still, how-to guides for the internet remained common in trade publications through the end of the decade, as journalists became more wary, too, of the veracity of online information. Tom Rosenstiel, the noted American journalism ethicist, warned that "the technology that has brought new voices into the media also can lower the standards of the press. And in its inevitable habit of magnification, that change in standards also changes how America sees itself."[28]

A move toward more sophisticated use of the internet—with some doubts

By the end of the 1990s and at the start of the 2000s, newsroom use of the internet grew more sophisticated as the larger public became more advanced with its use. According to a lengthy 2001 report in *Quill*, "with Internet access nearly universal in American newsrooms, training has become the focus for journalists aiming to become—or help their peers become—more technology savvy." Indeed, "Skills that were considered exceptional five years ago are now more common."[29] But those skills and training for them could be erratic. Some efforts, such as those led by the National Institute for Computer-Assisted Reporting (NICAR), helped along with some internal programs at newspapers, but in many newsrooms one person would be given the broad job of training (all) their peers, sometimes on top of their other work, or interested reporters had to seek it out for themselves.[30]

The reality on the ground was messy. Jennifer LaFleur worked at NICAR as a trainer before moving onto the *St. Louis Post-Dispatch* as a CAR editor. She said that training every staff member in advanced CAR techniques and the use of the internet for reporting could actually be a wasteful exercise, since the skills were perishable and not every reporter needed or even wanted to learn those skills. Editor buy-in became more critical in those kinds of situations, as they knew which staff members might benefit the most from training and how to devote an already-finite amount of time and resources to it. At the *Chicago Tribune*, reporters were sent to NICAR "boot camps" that covered topics such as reporting the census, although results could be more mixed in the larger newsroom. One of the designated CAR-projects reporters at the paper, Michael Berens, said that just 10 percent of reporters at the paper know how to utilize spreadsheets, for example. In response, the paper had been trying to find a dedicated trainer-editor.[31]

At even prestigious national newsrooms such as at *The Washington Post*, training was hit or miss, with basic skills common but the need for more niche training, for tasks like people-finding and deciphering medical research, was lacking. The problem was much more acute at smaller, regional newsrooms, even those that had an otherwise good selection of talent to work with, such as the Annapolis, Maryland-based *Capital*, "18 reporters share access to five computers equipped with Netscape and Microsoft Internet Explorer," with most having received training in college—most were younger, but this kind of situation was not uncommon, with turnover acerbating the issue. That meant that at some smaller newspapers, such as the *Daily Hampshire Gazette*, located in Northampton, Massachusetts, about one CAR project could be completed every 30 days or so.[32]

The distinction between CAR and online-based reporting was becoming fuzzier by the end of the 1990s and at the start of the 2000s. That led even some CAR advocates like Diane Weeks, who worked as the deputy information technology editor at *The Washington Post*, to admit that while "in the early days, Internet research was considered one of the arms of computer-assisted reporting . . . now, it's just considered a tool for reporting." CAR pioneer Bruce

Figure 4.1 Front page of Mediainfo.com

Source: Front page of *Mediainfo.com*, a limited-run publication by *Editor & Publisher*, April 1999.

Garrison had completed a survey of newspapers of 20,000 or more circulation, in which he found that in 1994, some 57 percent of news workers were using some kind of internet resource; within four years, or the end of 1998, that number had jumped to 95 percent, and would soon hit nearly 100 percent, if it had not already. Yahoo! and Alta Vista were favored search engines (while Google *was* around, again, it was just one among many other such search tools).[33]

Nora Paul, another CAR advocate who worked at the time as head of the University of Minnesota's Institute for New Media Studies, and before that, at Poynter, noted that even combined, these search engines reached less than 25 percent of the then-total-existing content online, and that journalists thus needed more training in how best to dig deeper into web resources. "For the most part, journalists don't get much training. . . . Which is a big issue and is not a new issue."[34]

That tendency to just go straight "to Google and type that in and run with it" was even then already ingrained in reporters, complained NICAR's training director, Tom McGinty; it was his mission to teach reporters to conduct more advanced searches that looked for specific terms and used specific databases. Both Paul and McGinty called for more serious reflection on the trustworthiness of online sources, while also not losing sight of the potential of internet-based information for reporting. Paul said that the guiding question should remain, with contemplating the veracity of online sources: "Who are these people and why are they telling me this?"[35]

Larger newsrooms, including the aforementioned *Chicago Tribune* and *Washington Post*, were beefing up their reporters' online access with faster connections and with specialized programs such as updated versions of Microsoft Access and Excel, but also SAS, used for statistics, and FoxPro, used for databases, and dedicating specialized workstations that had more memory, as needed. The latter paper also equipped many of their reporters' computers with the Dow Jones Archives and Nexis-Lexis.[36]

While that kind of support was not universal, reporters were no longer expected to pay for their own email access via AOL. Still, many smaller newsrooms had to share limited access and resources, including databases, even as web browsers and work-email accounts were much more common than even a decade prior. *The San Jose Mercury News* had been a pioneer in that kind of installation. Before, Paul had noted that the idea of placing only a few internet-wired computers in a newsroom, until the mid-1990s a common practice, was "like having a phone booth in the middle of the newsroom" (which had, in fact, been common, even if the booth was placed at the edge of a newsroom—eventually most reporters had their own phones, though that took until the 1920s and even the 1930s).[37]

Garrison agreed, noting that day-to-day use of the internet had gone from something like less than 33 percent in 1994 to 63 percent in 1998, echoing society's own adoption of the internet. Also, he observed that "as local, state and federal governments increased their own use of the web at the end of the 1990s, newspapers began to find the web more valuable and, in many cases, more user-friendly for retrieval of information."[38]

Email in the newsroom, and outside of it

While news workers had, of course, interacted with readers before, via letters to the editor, phone conversations or when out in public doing their reporting, the internet brought new avenues of engagement and an immediacy not felt before by either group. The larger topic of reader engagement online is beyond this focused study, but this researcher and a colleague are working on related projects that will hopefully unpack the moving target of greater engagement with people consuming the news online.[39]

That being said, one online tool used in newsrooms that deserves a closer look is electronic mail, i.e., email, which existed before the commercial internet and fascinated not just journalists but also the business world and, before that, military and civilian researchers alike, in Europe, the US and elsewhere.[40]

It should be noted at the outset that email was sometimes initially thought of as supplementary to other avenues of analog and digital communication. That included bulletin boards and other kinds of digital forums. Nora Paul, the CAR advocate, noted that "this private correspondence capability is the perfect way to contact and arrange to interview someone whose comments you might have read in the public posted message area," illustrating this early understanding of email as one among several ways of communicating with colleagues and readers alike.[41] On a related note, email was not necessarily free or easy to access, or easy to use, as has been noted previously. In fact, some journalists listed both their email addresses, but also their CompuServe handles, as a way to get a hold of them.[42]

Jack Lail, the metro editor of the *Knoxville News-Sentinel* and chair of the Society of Professional Journalists' New Information Technologies Committee, observed as early as the January/February 1994 issue of *Quill* that "email to the editor" could function as an early bulletin board system (BBS) offshoot. And while many newspapers opted to let Prodigy, AOL or CompuServe build their sites (and run them, for a share of the *potential* profits, as noted earlier in this chapter), some, like the "Electronic Trib" edition of *The Albuquerque Tribune*, or the Raleigh-based *News & Observer*, the *San Jose Mercury News, The New York Times* and *The Washington Post* all tried to foster online communities of various kinds, including, in some cases, message boards and other kinds of services. *USA Today* worked with CompuServe to create its USA Today Information Network. That service, in turn, relied on the Mosaic browser, and its graphical user interface (GUI).

USA Today offered email as part of its early online subscription package in the spring of 1995. For $14.95 a month, a user had up to three hours of online time, with each hour after that costing $3.95 (per hour); other services would charge similar amounts during this era.[43] While many other first-generation newspaper sites were static, these represented a minority that were far more dynamic than most of their peers in the mid-1990s, sometimes aggressively engaging with readers and inviting them to "talk" via email and other digital means with their reporters and editors.[44]

One model for how that might work was talk radio, with newspapers starting "electronic" versions, of themselves, in some cases, wanting to reclaim their traditional role of public-community forum from the upstart call-in shows then gaining popularity in the US. Barry Hollander, an assistant professor of journalism at the University of Georgia, estimated there were about "40 or so electronic versions of newspapers floating around in cyberspace" in the summer of 1994, and so this aspiration was off to a modest start.[45] In his analysis, Hollander claimed that readers "are less interested in 'reading' the electronic news than in talking with each other and those reporters and editors who put together the news." He related an anecdote, to reinforce his larger point:

> *An editor recently said that among the most popular features of his electronic newspaper was the Friday evening social gatherings in cyberspace, what he laughingly referred to as 'date night.' . . . electronic newspapers offer people the chance to be heard above and beyond simple letters to the editor . . . . These 'threads' may go on for some time . . . . While discussion can get at times downright nasty (called flaming), it provides an open forum, a two-way communication. Political leaders as well as newspaper staff may participate . . . . This is where newspapers and journalists must pay attention . . . . People want to be heard. They want to ask questions. And they want to talk to each other.*[46]

This two-way interaction manifested in forums, and in the ways that readers could directly write to reporters, instead of just the newspaper itself, via email. This applied to the creators of syndicated material, such as cartoonists.[47] Other early email experiments by newspapers including the printing of an email-address directory, as with the *Pottsville Republican*, in Pottsville, Pennsylvania, which published 250 as part of a 992-page phonebook.[48] Other publications experimented with entirely emailed editions, including the *Christian Science Monitor*, which, for $5 a month, tried to get at readers with slow internet.[49]

The conversation about how best to utilize email in the newsroom was tied to debates over free content, including emailed editions of even such prestige papers as the *New York Times*, a customized version of which could cost, before an early attempt at a paywall was dropped, as much as $49.95 a year. That version was delivered through Netscape Navigator 3.0's "InBox," which allowed for live HTML links, and let users email a whole web page, in some cases with Java applets, plug-ins and graphics, video and sound (though usually just text).[50]

Press releases, which drove (and still drive) news coverage, were increasingly delivered via email in the 1990s, with one survey of 600 newspapers and magazine editors revealing that 200 of them went online every day, for their work, with only 13 saying they did not have online access by early 1997.[51] This again reflected broader trends, with another study showing that about 31.3 million Americans of adult age were going online, with up to 45 million by 1998; 27 million were directly accessing the internet and 9.8 million under-18-year-olds were going online, with 5.7 at home and 4.1 at school. A total of 66 percent were looking for news, with 62 percent looking for info on hobbies, 56 on travel, 50 on government and community, 46 on health and medical and 41 percent on music and sports. Some 60 percent checked email daily, with 50 percent going online at least once a day in general.[52] Younger people in particular—some 83 percent, by one estimate—were going online on a daily basis, with email as the most-used application.[53] By the summer of 1999, an *Editor & Publisher* survey of 53,000 people from 75 newspaper sites showed that 82 percent checked newspapers almost as much as they checked their email (91 percent), with 72 percent going to news sites for local news, 40 percent for weather, 39 for national news and 38 for classified ads.[54]

But as a reminder that email access as we know it was not common, per se, even at otherwise tech-savvy newsrooms such as at the Sacramento, California, *Bee*, the ability to read attachments was hit or miss, depending on what kind of software was installed in the workstations.[55] Still, it was felt that increased email use, including the placing of email addresses next to bylines or at the ends of stories, encouraged "bonding and loyalty" with readers.[56]

Columnists, perhaps because they were primed to engage with their readers, tended to be fans of that form of communication. Mark Lane, who wrote for the *Daytona News-Journal* in Florida and for the Cox News Service, claimed that "email lets you know when you've succeeded in writing a column that speaks to your readers—and lets you know the day it appears. . . . You can't help but benefit from that." It also gave him a better idea of what editors at other papers were wanting from him.[57]

Emails and interviews

In one specific area, the emailed interview, journalism practices evolved in ways that paralleled that of the telephone a generation before. Both seasoned practitioners and journalism educators alike were skeptical that one could trust who was on the other side of the line. It was important to be questioning, they would argue, and to try to interview someone first in person, and second over the phone, and only lastly solely by email (scheduling an interview or clarifying some fact seemed fine).[58] This topic fascinated many writers in the journalism trade press, and so the use of email remained a popular topic in special sections throughout the late 1990s and into the 2000s, even as blogging and mobile journalism gradually led to an acceptance of the practice of emailing questions to subjects.

Some of the main concerns about emailed interviews centered around ideas of authority and attribution, but there were some advantages, like avoiding public-relations intermediaries and, of course, having parts of your story written for you without having to spend time typing up notes (or cleaning up notes typed while interviewing someone over the phone). Still, it was argued, not being physically present with someone or at least hearing the sound of their voice was considered a bad practice, as you could not as readily get a sense of the whole person. A phone call was a close second to being in person for an interview, in contrast. As the Long Island, New Jersey-based *Newsday* reporter Ed Lempinen put it, "you can hear the cadence, tone, pauses. You can hear whether the person is comfortable or at ease or excited, you can hear sorrow, you can hear laughter or anger, all in a range of subtle tones." In contrast, only emoticons were available to an email interviewer.[59]

Over time, some journalists and journalism educators changed their minds about the utility of the emailed interview, including Ken Metzler, who dismissed the practice in 1993, only to gradually embrace it through the decade. "There are many, many problems, but email is a good tool," he told a reporter for SPJ's *Quill* in 2005. "Its advantages outweigh its disadvantages."[60] One survey of journalists in 2000 saw growing acceptance of the practice by rank-and-file news workers, along with a similar study in 2001, by CAR advocate Bruce Garrison. He "found that 6.5 percent of interviews were conducted using e-mail, and 90 percent of the journalists surveyed considered the interviews 'successful' or 'very successful.'" Non-English speakers appreciated the ability to respond without having to be perfect in the fast give-and-take of American-style interviews. Time-zone differences and problems with scheduling were eased with the ability to send asynchronous messages, and wary sources could be coaxed to write versus speak live over a phone, as was the case for a story on hacking online banks.[61]

Some news organizations, including *The Spokesman-Review* in Washington state, compiled email directories, using the contact information of people who had written letters to the editor. Some 6,500 were eventually added, providing a helpful pool of people for commentary, by either email or phone. The Associated Press, inspired by this, launched its Reader-Interactive Program, which established similar email directories at 60 newspapers in the US. That had a secondary effect of helping beat reporters cultivate sources more deeply, especially in the business and technology industries.[62]

Still, as is the case with any new journalism-technology tool, some skeptics remained convinced that email was something to be wary of, again reflecting the long process by which the use of the telephone became fully acceptable, even after it had won over some early critics.[63] Email was felt to be less spontaneous, and possibly less truthful. Relying on email also led reporters to stay stuck in the newsrooms, and not get out and physically interact with sources, and let newspapers' owners find excuses to cut payroll at a moment when concerns about staffing were growing.

Michael Bugeja, who worked as the director of the Greenlee School of Journalism and Communication at Iowa State University at the time, and who often wrote columns for journalism trade magazines, claimed that critical scoops could be lost if all reporters did was email their sources, including how a reporter discovered problems with the swine-flu vaccination rollout in 1976. He argued that previous communication technologies had taken reporters away from non-journalists, and not in good ways. As he put it, "community matters. . . . Reporting matters. . . . The Internet used in tandem with face-to-face reporting is paramount in our time. But are we adequately portraying to employees when we should and should not use technology? About how to use the Internet and e-mail effectively in concert with the legwork standards of yore?"[64]

Other critics felt that younger reporters in particular picked up bad habits fast with new technologies (again, as with the telephone), such as the then-popular instant messenger apps like those found on AOL, Yahoo! Chat and MSN Messenger.[65] Training was spotty, however, on the use of both these apps and emailing, and varied dramatically from newspaper to newspaper. This was despite noted examples of even vaunted news organizations like the AP falling for email hoaxes, including a famous 2003 case in which a New Hampshire man falsely claimed that he was a terrorist from Pakistan.[66]

Other concerns were focused on the need for the due diligence required of reporters, including taking information from online sources without getting their permission first. Spelling, grammar and thus clarity could suffer from sloppy use of emails or lazy attributions more generally.[67] This researcher once warned his colleagues at a student-run newspaper in the United Kingdom that taking "quotes" from a source's Facebook page without permission was probably not a great idea; ultimately, the source threatened to sue the paper until it apologized, which it did, narrowly avoiding libel litigation.[68]

More issues with email, even as newsrooms became more comfortable with online tools, involved the writing of true-but-still-too-vague responses from interview subjects, or the ways that emails made it more challenging to ask follow-up questions in some circumstances. And again, the lack of witnessed, sensory details—of what a place or even a person smelled, sounded and looked like—made emailed interviews less attractive to some reporters. Not every interview subject had access to a computer, or to email, through the 1990s and into the 2000s, especially in the developing world—in other words, e-mail was not ubiquitous for a long time.[69]

Still, email allowed reporters, some argued, to regain lost time, and, ironically, get back outside and talk to people face to face. Emailed requests for interviews were thought of as a positive way to begin an interaction, instead of a voicemail or a cold call. They could just complement an in-person or phoned interview, especially with tough topics such as personal relationships. Best practices with emailing, circa 2005, involved:

- the use of a professional, versus a personal account
- a clearly expressed reason for contacting someone, with qualifications and credentials
- how one acquired someone's email address, and/or why their perspective was important
- an explicit reminder that email responses might get published verbatim
- brevity
- open-ended questions
- how to write back
- one's contact information, including phone number, and an offer to talk via that medium
- asking for full names and ways for the subject to confirm who one was, from their side
- running emails through a spellcheck program
- avoiding attachments
- knowing one's email could be read by anyone
- following up as needed.[70]

The use of email raised some novel legal questions, at least at the time, and so that remained a consideration. Emailed questions could help fight mistakes with quotations and show how the reporter worked to fairly use a source's perspective, but that could work against a reporter. It was best to think of them as one would regard story notes, argued Paul Bargren, a lawyer specializing in media law, and who worked in the Milwaukee office of Foley & Lardner LLP. That meant that comments or callous remarks were part of the record, too. Internal emails in a newsroom could be treated as legally binding. They were possibly permanent, Bargren noted, and that meant that issues of confidentiality could be tricky. "E-mail provides lots of benefits . . . but it has drawbacks as well."[71]

Conclusion

When thinking about how the internet changed journalism in the US, Canada and the UK in the mid-to-late 1990s, it is important to think about how much journalism did *not* change, at least not yet. Stories were still written physically in big metro newsrooms and edited by comprehensive and well-funded staffs—layoffs loomed large in the near future, but were not there yet.[72] Despite costly and rarely recouped investments, media companies still maintained healthy profit margins, even as their readers aged and online ad revenue was starting to slip. And while it was disastrous to some companies, the online bubble's bursting did not derail overall investment in online journalism.[73]

As has been noted before, this is not a business history of the newspaper industry, but its financial state *did* drive a great deal of the reactive decision making of the late 1990s and early 2000s about the internet, and often in short-sighted (at least to us, looking back) directions. And so it makes sense, when reflecting on this era, to remember that comparative financial stability meant that the slow evolution of newsroom practices—not a rapid revolution—tended to be the norm and not the other way around. The use of email followed previous patterns set by the telephone, and the ways databases and experts were consulted and featured—even if in somewhat novel ways, such as live question-and-answer sessions, in the latter case—reinforced and not upended how things had been done before. As Boczkowski has argued, newspaper culture could be both innovative and not, at the same time, in the form of its still-new web-based content and storytelling.

But as the decade passed, and social media arrived on the scene, initially in the form of Facebook and blogs, and followed by apps such as Twitter and, still later, Facebook's photographic cousin, Instagram, many industry watchers fretted more about the long-term financial survivability of not just the *printed* news, but original reporting online more broadly. The next chapter continues to explore how the newsroom evolved with the internet (and sometimes did not), as "Web 2.0" tools—focused around the concept of "interactivity"—arrived on the scene by the end of the 2000s.[74] It explores how blogging, particularly the kind that made use of original reporting, impacted newsrooms as they increasingly focused their attention on the internet. Finally, it looks at how ideas of "portable" reporting helped to inspire a shift to "mobile" journalism. All these changes, in the lead up to the 2008 financial crisis, led to a deepening sense of catastrophe with the internet's impact on the journalism industry.

Notes

1 Chapter 2 (briefly) examined how Rogers' diffusions theory has been adopted by journalism studies scholars such as Ángel Arrese. Chapter 3 similarly looked at how "disruption" has to be handled carefully, and in the introduction, and Chapter 1 touched on how ideas of materiality and technology adoption go together (or should).

2 Pablo Boczkowski, *Digitizing the News: Innovation in Online Newspapers* (Cambridge, MA: MIT Press, 2005), 51, 52–55.

3 Ibid., 44–48.

4 Ibid., 49, 55–64, 69.

5 Ibid., 70–72. "This mix of success and failure loses its seemingly contradictory character in light of newspapers' culture of innovation: failures online usually meant that print was in good health—at least in the short run—but this, in turn, limited actors' ability to pursue more offensive and longer term strategies with higher risks but potentially higher returns."

6 Citing a variety of primary sources (many of which are also examined here), Boczkowski points out that "profitability was a particularly sensitive issue for online newspapers," with display ads, sponsors, classified ads, directors, internet services, subscriptions, some on-site transactions, and initial attempts at paying for individuals stories all bringing in subpar income. In fact, 90 percent of American newspapers lost money on internet ventures in 1996, and 1998-era investments were spectacularly bad, even by the largesse of the time. In that latter year, Knight Ridder lost $23 million, the New York Times Co. lost somewhere between $10 and 15 million, the Tribune Co. some $35 million, and Times Mirror $20 million—see Boczkowski, 67, but also, Robert Neuwirth, "Race into Cyberspace Gushes $80 Million [in] Red Ink," *Editor & Publisher*, December 19, 1998, 12–13. Boczkowski is correct, in this researcher's view, in excepting both *The Wall Street Journal* and *The Washington Post* from the general trend in the late 1990s and early 2000s, however, with both sites managing to make profits (though how much remains somewhat unclear) for their owners. This was due to the former's paywall and unique mission and the latter's similarly unique purview, as well as heavy investment in original content. And while it is hard to determine how well British and Canadian papers fared during this era, it is probable that big brands such as *The Guardian* and the BBC News were able to more or less break even, while smaller, more regional and local papers struggled to afford the costs of online conversions. See Boczkowski, *Digitizing the News*, 200.

7 C. W. Anderson, *Apostles of Certainty: Data journalism and the Politics of Doubt* (New York: Oxford University Press, 2018).

8 For more on this topic, see Perry Parks and Will Mari, "Teaching CAR: The Computer-Assisted Reporting Movement in Journalism Textbooks, c. 1980–2010," an article under review at the time of this book's writing. See also Philip

Meyer, *Precision Journalism: A Reporter's Introduction to Social Science Methods* (Bloomington, IN: Indiana University Press).

9 Margaret DeFleur, *Computer-Assisted Investigative Reporting: Development and Methodology* (Mahwah, NJ: Lawrence Erlbaum Associates, Publishers, 1997); for more on the legacy of CAR, see Anderson, 2018.

10 Starting in 1994, some 3.8 million people were online, or about 17 percent of American households with computers (which, in turn, was about 24 percent of all Americans). See Boczkowski, *Digitizing the News*, 35. By 1999, national newspapers in the US were achieving unique online visitor numbers that approached that of their print products. For more on this topic, see previous chapters. For these estimates, however, see Boczkowski, *Digitizing the News*, 50; Benjamin Compaine, "The Online Information Industry," in *Who Owns the Media: Competition and Concentration in the Mass Media Industry*, eds. Benjamin Compaine and Douglas Gomery (Mahwah, NJ: Erlbaum, 2000).

11 Bruce Garrison, "Newsgathering Tool of the 1990s: There Are a Number of News Organizations Where Computer-Assisted Reporting Is a Significant Part of Daily Reporting and Not Being Reserved Just for Special Projects," *Editor & Publisher*, June 24, 1995, 16, 123. Garrison was a prolific CAR author and promoter. His work was excerpted in *Editor & Publisher*, along with other CAR writers, and became almost a kind of beat or genre.

12 Shawn McIntosh, "CAJ's Dirty Secrets: Don't Let the Hype Fool You—It's Hard Work," *Quill*, September 1993, 23.

13 John S. Makulowich, "Internet: Explore the 'Network of Networks,' and Email: Make Contact Without Playing Fun Tag," *Quill*, September 1993, 27–28.

14 Arik Hesseldahl, "After the Hack: Questions Follow the *Times* Attack," *Columbia Journalism Review*, January–February 1999, 14; John Annese, "The Digital Watercooler Gets Hot," *Columbia Journalism Review*, January–February 1999, 14; see also "About IRE," *Investigative Reporters and Editors Inc.*, accessed September 8, 2021, www.ire.org/about-ire/.

15 John Annese, "The Digital Watercooler Gets Hot," *Columbia Journalism Review*, January–February 1999, 14.

16 Makulowich, "Internet," 27–28. Makulowich, in turn, cites, Michael Strangelove and Diane Kovacs, "Directory of Electronic Journals, Newsletters and Academic Discussion Lists," *Quill*, September 1993, 29.

17 Forbush was associate vice president for university affairs at State University of New York at Stony Brook. With 20–30 queries daily, ProfNet was designed to help answer niche questions about everything from frostbite in birds (why they don't get it), South American winds, aromatherapy, "older women in prison," and economic predictions for British Columbia, according to Forbush. See Strangelove and Kovacs, "Directory of Electronic Journals, Newsletters and Academic Discussion Lists," 29.

18 Makulowich, "Internet," 27–28. Bill Kovach, then an assistant professor at Radford University, is quoted here.

19 Makulowich, "Internet," 27–28. It should be worth noting that according to Makulowich, the CARR-L had about 366 active users in September 1993, from 19 countries. He also bases some of his estimates on industry data, though the provenance of that data is unclear. NICAR's listserv had about 400 subscribers to its "Uplink" newsletter in May 1995, with the parent organization funded at least partially by a $221,000 grant from the Freedom Forum; see William Webb, "Resource File on Database Reporting," *Editor & Publisher*, May 15, 1995, 35.

20 Makulowich, "Internet," 27–28.

21 See, for example, Mark Fitzgerald, "Losing Access to Public Records: Government Trend to Charge More and More for Its Electronic Records Is Hampering the Public's Ability to Acquire Them," *Editor & Publisher*, May 15, 1993, 9.

22 William Webb, "Unlocking Data Power: Database Reporting Boosts Traditional Journalism and Builds Foundation for Digitized Papers of the Future," *Editor & Publisher*, May 15, 1995, 32–35, 41; see also Estes Thompson, "McClatchy to Buy the News & Observer of Raleigh," *Associated Press*, May 17, 1995, https://apnews.com/article/4bb031aea8b9d427b34f37dfeeff4ae2.

23 David Noack, "Newsroom Intranets: Like Corporations, News Organizations Are Beginning to Realize That the World Wide Web's Structure Is Perfectly Suited for Use in Closed Internal Networks That Connect Reporters to Vast Troves of Useful Information," *Editor & Publisher*, June 1997, 22–24.

24 B. G. Yovovich, "'Pushing' the Newsroom: New Online Tracking Tools Enhance Reporting—Cover a Beat? Imagine Having a Personal Assistant Automatically Foraging Through Vast Quantities of Online News, Corporate Information and Government Data to Keep You Up to Date on the Latest Happenings Everywhere, Everyday," *Editor & Publisher*, June 1997, 30–32.

25 For more on the history of CMS, which is beyond the scope of this book, see Juliette De Maeyer, "Content Management Systems and Journalism," in *Oxford Research Encyclopedia of Communication* (Oxford: Oxford University Press, 2019), accessed September 8, 2021, https://oxfordre.com/communication/view/10.1093/acrefore/9780190228613.001.0001/acrefore-9780190228613-e-792.

26 Charles Bowen, "Reporter's Digital How-to: Following the Money Trail: New Election Fund-Tracking Site a Potent Tool for Journalists," *Editor & Publisher*, March 14, 1998, 46–47.

27 Keith Shelton, "Lone Star CAR: Texas Newspapers Harness Computers for News Research," *Editor & Publisher*, January 24, 1998, 23.

28 Adam Gaffin, "Cybernavigation Not for the Faint of Heart: New Tools Make Getting Around [the] Internet a Bit Easier for Newcomers," *Quill*, November–December 1994, 18–19.

29 Michelle Johnson, "Keeping the Newsroom Current: Hi-tech Reporting Tools Are More Available, but Training Plans Vary Among Media Outlets," *Quill*, May 2001, 25–28.

30 Ibid.

31 Ibid.

32 Ibid.

33 Ibid; Garrison was a professor who taught journalism at the University of Miami at the time.

34 Johnson, "Keeping the Newsroom Current," 25–28; also see "Nora Paul," accessed September 9, 2021, https://worldpressinstitute.org/board/nora-paul/.

35 Johnson, "Keeping the Newsroom Current," 25–28; it should be noted that long before our current "fake news" debates, at least as early as special issues in *Editor & Publisher* in 1998, worries about "fake news," called as such, were present in journalism's trade publications.

36 Johnson, "Keeping the Newsroom Current," 25–28.

37 Ibid; see also Will Mari, "Technology in the Newsroom: Adoption of the Telephone and the Radio Car from c. 1920 to 1960," *Journalism Studies* 19, no. 9 (2018): 1366–89.
38 Johnson, "Keeping the Newsroom Current," 25–28.
39 Some of this is discussed in my previous book, *A Short History of Disruptive Journalism Technologies: 1960–1990* (Abingdon, UK: Routledge, 2019). For more on this topic, see "(Electronic) Mailing the Editor: Emails, Message Boards and Early Interactive Web Design in the 1990s," which was under review at the time of this book's writing. Finally, for more on email as part of the CAR movement, see work by Perry Parks and I that will soon be under review at the time of this manuscript's writing.
40 For an example of an early book on the topic, see Stephen Connell and Ian A. Galbraith, *Electronic Mail: A Revolution in Business Communications* (New York: Van Nostrand Reinhold Company, Inc., 1980).
41 Nora Paul, "Database & Bulletin Board Services: A Guide to On-line Resources," *Quill*, September 1993, 18–20.
42 Chuck Taylor, "Navigating Cyberspace: On-line Services Try to Make World Discovery into Child's Play," *Quill*, March 1995, 20–23. Taylor, then a reporter at *The Seattle Times* who covered "electronic media, including television, radio, cable, and commercial on-line information services," for example, listed at the end of his story an early email address ("ctay-new@seatimes.com"), as well as his CompuServe (BBS?) locator ("71460,1463"), and his America Online handle ("ChckTylr"), wrote a kind to the early Web for reporters, highlighting the merits of AOL vs. CompuServe, GENie and Prodigy, along with email and how to get access to it. See also Joe Abernathy, "Casting the Internet: A New Tool for Electronic Newsgathering," *Columbia Journalism Review*, January–February 1993, 56. Abernathy wrote for the Houston Chronicle as a special-projects desk reporter; he lists his CompuServe address (73060,3343) and his early email address, joe.abernathy@chron.com; he also invites people to send him an envelope that was pre-stamped if you wanted a list of internet service providers.
43 Anonymous Staff Writer, "USA Today Makes Online Debut," *Editor & Publisher*, May 15, 1995, 35.
44 Jack Lail, "Newspapers On-line: Electronic Delivery Is Hot . . . Again," *Quill*, January–February 1994, 39–44.
45 Barry Hollander, "Talk Radio, Videotext, and the Information Superhighway," *Editor & Publisher*, July 16, 1994, 60, 51.
46 Ibid., 60.
47 David Astor, "Email Is Hailed by Creators Who Used It," *Editor & Publisher*, May 6, 1995, 38–40.
48 "E-mail Directory," *Editor & Publisher*, March 23, 1996, 53.
49 Steve Outing, "Worldwide Email Edition," *Editor & Publisher*, January 25, 1997, 26.
50 Jodi B. Cohen, "Browsers and Newspapers," *Editor & Publisher*, September 21, 1996, 30; to be clear, *The New York Times* was also offering large portions of its site for free at this point, as most newspapers shifted to providing free first, in an attempt to capture advertisers versus subscribers.
51 "Internet Routine for the Newsroom," *Editor & Publisher*, March 8, 1997, 49.
52 John Consoli, "Online Usage: 'More Than a Fad:' Survey Finds 50% of Users Log on Daily; Most Seek News," *Editor & Publisher*, August 9, 1997, 26.

Also telling: 36 percent clicked on online ads, with steady use increasing (with 4–5 million news users a year).

53 Scott Kirsner, "Most Heavily Wired Readers: Students—A New Study Finds That Cyberspace Is Rapidly Enveloping Every Aspect of College Life. Are Newspapers Missing an Opportunity?" *Editor & Publisher*, October 11, 1997, 34–35.

54 Joe Strupp, "Welcomed Visitors: *E&P* Study Shows Newspaper Web Sites Busier Than Ever, But Still Learning the Ropes," *Editor & Publisher*, July 3, 1999, 22–23, 26–27.

55 Ken Liebeskind, "Recruiting in Cyberspace: Newspapers Begin Trolling the Web for the Perfect Match of Job to Employee," *Editor & Publisher*, November 22, 1997, 17–18.

56 Carl Sullivan, "Newspapers Get Mixed Report Card from Consultant," *Editor & Publisher*, December 26, 1998, 19.

57 Dave Astor, "Energized by Inbox: Columnists Learn the Joy of Email: Many Say the Technology, Now Popular for a Decade, Helps Them Do a Better Job Than When Post Letters Were King," *Editor & Publisher*, August 2004, 46.

58 Russell Frank, "You've Got Quotes! While e-mail Can Be a Valuable Reporting Tool, It Often Falls Short of Other Interview Techniques," *Quill*, October 1999, 18–22.

59 Ibid. Lempinen went on to write for Salon.com, where he presumably conducted his fair share of email-reliant interviews. See "Edward Lempinen," *Greater Good*, accessed September 10, 2021, https://greatergood.berkeley.edu/profile/edward_lempinen.

60 Bonnie Bressers, "Mixed Message: Experts Debate Use of Email as Interviewing Tool," *Quill*, March 2005, 10–14.

61 Ibid.

62 Ibid. The original program was started by Ken Sands, "managing editor of online and new media," at *The Spokesman-Review*.

63 For more on the slow adoption of the telephone as a reporting tool, see Will Mari, *The American Newsroom: A History, 1920–1960* (Columbia, MO: University of Missouri Press, 2021).

64 Bressers, "Mixed Message," 10–14.

65 Trushar Barot and Eytan Oren, "Guide to Chat Apps," *Tow Center for Digital Journalism*, November 9, 2015, accessed September 11, 2021, www.cjr.org/tow_center_reports/guide_to_chat_apps.php#key-players-and-case-studies.

66 Bressers, "Mixed Message," 10–14.

67 Ibid.

68 To be clear, this incident happened in 2010, and concerned social media, and not bulletin boards and forums, which were still a gray area in the early 2000s.

69 Bressers, "Mixed Message," 10–14.

70 "The following suggestions for conducting email interviews are offered by journalists who use email for interviewing under certain circumstances, including Doug Daniel, Washington, DC-based journalist and freelancer, and Sandeep Junnarkar, Weil Visiting Professor at the School of Journalism at Indiana University-Bloomington." Bonnie Bressers, "E-mail Interviewing Tips," *Quill*, March 2005, 12.

71 Bonnie Bressers, "Legal Ramifications of e-mail Interviews," *Quill*, March 2005, 13.

72 For more on the idea that newsroom culture was both innovation and, a bit paradoxically, slow to change and even somehow stubborn to change, see Boczkowski, *Digitizing the News*.

73 A history of that moment is a bit beyond the scope of this study, but is worthy of a separate project or projects.

74 For more on this argument, please see "(Electronic) Mailing the Editor: Emails, Message Boards and Early Interactive Web Design in the 1990s," which was under review at the time of this book's writing.

5 The internet and newsgathering in the mid-to-late 2000s

The 2000s was the decade when journalism finally fully faced the internet, not as some sort of mortal enemy, but as a more fully fleshed out delivery platform and as a recurring challenge for its predominately ad-based business model. No longer would "reach before revenue" work as well.[1] This was all in the context of increasing internet use in the daily lives of news consumers.

In 2000, some 52 percent of adult Americans used the internet; by 2010 that number was 76 percent.[2] Those numbers were similar in Canada, where 51 percent of Canadian households had access to the internet in 2000; in 2010, that number was 79 percent.[3] In the United Kingdom, that number had gone from about a third of all Britons in 2000 to nearly two-thirds in 2007 and 2011.[4] Those numbers belie inequalities of access, including those based on socioeconomic factors, age, gender and geography, but the context is key—newsrooms and news workers were living in an increasingly wired world, with everything from banking to car buying to dating far more normalized as online activities at the end of the decade than they were at the beginning.

That matters because the slow-but-steady, conservatively innovative, online adoptions of the late 1990s and early 2000s, and discussed in the previous chapter, began to be less-than-fast-enough by the mid-to-late 2000s. To put it another way, the pace of internet time changed had changed, or at least the perception of it, to borrow from media historian David Karpf.[5]

New approaches and threats alike sprouted with vigor in the 2000s, from news-blogging to mobile journalism to debates about paywalls (or the lack thereof). These developments, especially the first two, will be the primary focus of this chapter, with the emphasis remaining on rank-and-file reporters and editors and how they thought of, and reacted to, the continued rise of the internet as a cultural, political and economic force.[6]

DOI: 10.4324/9780429324871-5

Online journalism at the start of the decade

The events of September 11, 2001, and online coverage of them, seemed to catalyze conversations among industry observers, scholars and journalists themselves about the role of the internet in their reporting. Unlike television and radio, internet commentary and analysis seemed to borrow—in its better moments—from the traditions of print journalism.

Writing from the perspective of the UK, Stuart Allan identifies 9/11 as a significant turning point for online newsgathering, showcasing both the vulnerabilities and possibilities of this new-old form of delivering stories. Heavy traffic and the technical limitations of dial-up connections, still then prevalent, meant that for some users, the experience of reading about 9/11 was a frustrating one, Allan noted.[7] Most readers relied on TV and radio for breaking news coverage, with even CNN.com having to resort to a bare-bones version to keep up with demand.[8]

But a kind of "personal journalism," i.e., "citizen-produced" (sometimes called user-generated, storytelling) emerged in the wake of the attacks, on early weblogs, i.e., "blogs" by both amateurs and full-time journalists. In many ways, it supplemented, and not replaced the round-the-clock coverage by traditional outlets. Reporters sought out eyewitnesses in chatrooms and on forums, and some US network news organizations, such as ABC News, hosted online conversations, some of which devolved into bigotry but others providing important spaces for grieving, confused people to find trustworthy news.[9]

Americans also turned to the BBC News and *The Guardian* for information during 9/11, especially vía these and other international news organizations' web sites. Like in the US, some of these sites struggled to handle the millions of new "hits" from visitors, but the British outlets in particular formed a kind of bridge to the rest of the world, and vice versa.[10] Citing data from the Pew Internet and American Life Project, Allan noted that 36 percent of all internet users in the US had searched for news after the attacks, 29 percent on that Tuesday, September 11, representing some 30 million people (and thus more than one-third greater than usual).[11] Still, Allan, citing NYU-based journalism-studies scholar Jay Rosen, noted that while there was "plenty of journalism *on* the Internet. . . [v]ery little of it is *of* the Internet" [italics in original].[12]

Still, the presence of diverse points of view, and, when it eventually happened, more original reporting, showcased internet-based news as no longer a nice-to-have way of getting news, from the consumers' perspective, or of producing and publishing the news, from journalists' point of view.[13] It was into this new reality that the blogging phenomenon arrived.

The arrival of blogs

In both the mainstream and trade press, coverage of bloggers and blogging seems to have fascinated journalists more than the lay reader during the 2000s, but it is important to examine the reasons for this heightened interest.[14] And while a holistic history of blogging, per se, is beyond this brief book's strict focus, it is important to note that they arrived, as noted earlier, in the aftermath of 9/11 and a renewed focus on commentary by readers, in an internet environment that had "grown in recent years from a fringe cultural phenomenon to a significant site of cultural transformation and production in its own right."[15] As it concerns journalism, blogging arguably grew up with online news, or immediately alongside it.

With roots as varied (and murky) as The Whole Earth 'Lectric Link, i.e., "The Well," an early online community, and, later, updates to online publishing that included more user-friendly platforms such as Moveable Type, LiveJournal and WordPress, by the late 1990s, "blogging was somehow more personal and more purposeful than simply having a homepage. The whole point of having a blog was to share something with the world."[16] The resulting "blogosphere" thus encompassed everything from regular people logging their life's events to professional journalists who either established blogs as part of their work or blogged their way into more mainstream journalistic work, often through original reporting.[17] A classic case of the latter is media commentator Brian Stelter, who moved from his own blog to working for *The New York Times* and then CNN. As Stelter put it in an interview with *Politico*, "I coded my way in, back when coding just meant learning basic HTML. I built web sites starting around age 11. First about books, then about video games, then about TV news."[18]

As Dan Gillmor has noted, the 9/11 attacks had helped to create a new generation of avid bloggers-news workers, news junkies (or both) being among the more prolific.[19] They had "discovered the power of their publishing tool."[20] Among more rank-and-file journalists, the blogging phenomenon evolved from being seen as a kind of odd new threat, to perhaps more of an asset, but an undercurrent of anxiety wafted off of stories about it, in the first few years of the 2000s. Some outlets still referred to them as "Weblogs," and questioned their capacity to remain as ethical and detached as professional journalists' work in newsprint or at least on a sanctioned news site.[21]

Others waxed eloquent about blogs' capacity to reinvigorate a kind of 1960s-style counterculture of " 'underground' newspapers."[22] Matt Welch, an associate editor for *Reason* magazine and a co-founder of LAExaminer.com, "an interactive local news digest," attended the Association of Alternative Newsweeklies conference in San Francisco, but left unimpressed.

Instead, it was "blogging technology" that had "given the average Jane the ability to write, edit, design, and publish her own editorial product—to be read and responded to by millions of people, potentially—for around $0 to $200 a year. It has begun to deliver on some of the wild promises about the Internet that were heard in the 1990s. Never before have so many passionate outsiders . . . stormed the ramparts of professional journalism."[23]

Welch went on, describing bloggers as "connecting intimately with readers in a way reminiscent of old-style metro columnists or the liveliest of the New Journalists," digging into hyper-focused topics like "appellate court rulings, new media proliferation in Tehran, the intersection of hip-hop and libertarianism . . . and perhaps most excitingly of all, committing impressive, spontaneous acts of decentralized journalism."[24]

Blog platforms helped bring web publishing from being "theoretically possible and cheap" to being actually so, and he credits Pyra Labs, among other companies, with making that possible. Before, through the 1990s, to publish your own site, "you still had to learn HTML coding, which was inscrutable enough to make one long for the days of typesetting and paste-up." Blogging changed that, radically, by lowering the barriers to entry for the average person. By 2000, it was taking off enough to be featured in *The New Yorker*.[25]

Welch identified the online reaction to 9/11 as a key moment for both journalists and bloggers alike. Prolific writers inspired others, who linked to still others (linking aggressively being a hallmark of early blogging, to both other blogs and stories, as well as more traditional news sites). While not quite exponential, as the majority of blogs did not last beyond a few tentative posts, Welch describes how by the fall of 2003, Blogger could claim 1.5 million users, LiveJournal had some 1.2 million and some estimates put the figure overall somewhere "between 2.4 million and 2.9 million." He attributed their success to "personality, eyewitness testimony, editorial filtering, and uncounted gigabytes of new knowledge," identifying bloggers such as Elizabeth Spiers, Salam Pax and Steven Den Beste as blogging their way to freelancing or writing regularly for *The New York Times*, *The Guardian* and *The Wall Street Journal*, respectively.[26]

Blogging had the potential to hold mainstream journalism accountable, *and* empower journalists to specialize with their reporting, since "beat reporting is a natural fit for a blog—reporters can collect standing links to sites of interest, dribble out stories and anecdotes that don't necessarily belong in the paper, and attract a specific like-minded readership." The challenge for readers and news operations eager to hire bloggers would be in weeding out the "90 percent" of blogs that were not worth reading or were not maintained. Journalism would not be replaced by blogging, but it could be made better by it, seems to have been the tone of the coverage of the phenomenon in the first part of the 2000s.[27]

It could be crowdsourced, too. Chris Allbritton, an independent war correspondent who had worked for the AP, raised some $14,500 from 342 donors to cover the war in Iraq. According to Jay Rosen, who highlighted his work in a fall 2003 issue of *Columbia Journalism Review*, Allbritton used the money to get a "plane ticket to Turkey (where he snuck over the border and found the war), a laptop, a Global Positioning Satellite unit, a rented satellite phone, a digital camera and enough cash to move around, keep fed and buy his way out of trouble." With some 23,000 users, his site, www.back-to-iraq.com, Rosen argued, showed that a determined reporter could find an audience big enough to sustain expensive journalism, at least temporarily.[28]

By 2005, mainstream news sites were trying to make themselves "more blogger-friendly," featuring a select group of bloggers on their home pages (usually a showcase of the best work of the day, a digital "top of the fold," as it were). Even successful sites for publications such as *The Wall Street Journal* and *USA Today* were considering how to incorporate blogger-generated stories and commentary.[29] Another, more extensive effort took place at the *News & Record* in Greensboro, North Carolina. There the focus was on letting local bloggers take part in the paper's main site. The NYU's Jay Rosen said that "I've been waiting for this. . . . The organization willing to be a little radical," and Jack Shafer, who was then a blog critic and media-industry curmudgeon, agreed, "They're taking wondering first steps at trying to see, as newspapers become increasingly digitized, as the division between the print edition and the online edition evaporates even more, if there's something that compels people to come to the newspaper."[30] But other observers remained circumspect.

Bloggers remained primarily opinion-driven, riffing off already researched and in many cases published material, and only rarely their own original reporting. At their best, blogs could drive competition with journalists, but at worst, they lived off the latter's hard work.[31] "Reader blogs," so called because they were written by readers with more allegiance to the traditional print product, were a compromise, then, attempting to connect a newspaper to the popularity of blogs while retaining some control over the content. This was the case at large regional papers such as *The Seattle Times* and the Minneapolis *Star Tribune*. At the latter paper, a "new issues blog by staffer Eric Black called 'The Big Question' [included] discussions about stories of the day," including information on how they had been reported and became part of the paper's online coverage.[32]

Some sites, especially *The Huffington Post*, were initially entirely written by unpaid writers, with a small core of paid staff.[33] Others, curated by more mainstream newspapers, were pitched as local news "hubs," as was the case of the "reader-generated content" or "citizen journalism" site run by the

Rocky Mountain News and pitched as a network of neighborhood blogs. The latter generated a modest revenue for its parent paper, with about 309,000 page views per month from 45,000 visitors. The *Mountain News* wanted to syndicate this model, for between about $2,000 and $10,000 a month, depending on the size of the market. An initial network of 20 papers, including *The Knoxville News-Sentinel* in Tennessee, the LA Newspaper Group and the Scripps Treasure Coast Newspaper Group, expressed interest.[34]

Certain topics, like politics, seemed to lend themselves more readily to blogging than others.[35] High-school sports and other niche activities seemed tailored to the scale of blogging, at least as done by reporters as part of their other duties (including filing their daily quota of stories).[36] It was this latter, additional burden, that threatened to tire reporters out. As Renée Petrina, writing for *Quill* in the fall of 2004, noted, "There is a hunger for reliable information and for perspective. If you can deliver both, then you'll have a successful . . . blog. It's not that complex. But is difficult to do well day in and day out."[37]

In a long report on the state of blogging in 2005, also in *Quill*, their growing strengths (and more apparent weaknesses) were highlighted. Their usefulness in disasters was growing. After the devastating December 2004 tsunami in Southeast Asia, for example, bloggers filled news gaps with their initial reports, reinforcing their value to even well-resourced news organizations like *The New York Times*, BBC News and the *Christian Science Monitor*. One close blog-watcher, the managing producer of MSNBC.com, Jonathan Dube, said that more than 200 such organizations were reliant on blogs to some degree.[38]

The line between a "personal" and "professional" blog, though, remained fuzzy. Another journalistic-blog observer, Rebecca Blood, compared them to letter writing. She said that their relative useability—requiring no more than a basic grasp of how the internet worked—helped their popularity, and credited Blogger.com, started in the summer of 1999 by Evan Williams, Paul Bausch and Meg Hourihan, with part of that (the company was later sold to Google). Another important early blogging pioneer was Andrew Smales, who started Pitas.com, also in the summer of 1999, in Toronto. His Diaryland.com network became a kind of model for others to follow, with some 2 million people logging on by 2005. His strength—and the other sites' appeal that followed—was that you did not need to know how to code, or code very much, beyond, perhaps a rudimentary knowledge of HTML.[39]

Tech-commentator Dan Gillmor, ever aware of mid-2000s media-industry trends, called on journalists to read and write their own blogs, saying that they had "replaced trade magazines." Gillmor himself had run the SiliconValley.com blog before leaving *The San Jose Mercury News*.[40] And more generally, the practice of journalism did not seem under any actual threat from blogs alone, just perhaps from the business model (or lack of one) they hinted at.

Bloggers-as-aficionados made sense, some journalists believed, since many were, again, opinion-driven, or when they did their own reporting, were focused on niche issues or subjects, like technology and medicine. They could also exist in parallel with larger media operations, supplementing or commentating on their coverage, as with the Gothamist in New York City. As Jen Chung, the editor of the latter site put it, in 2005, "Blogs and newspapers are starting to feel comfortable with their relationship of feeding off each other . . . though perhaps it's a symbiotic relationship, not mutualistic."[41]

By the mid-2000s, blogs were becoming popular in journalism education as a way to teach the next generation of reporters to be more entrepreneurial and less reliant on traditional pathways into the field. It was thought to be a way to reach both young newsreaders and news workers, less accustomed to reading a print product and perhaps skeptical of dedicated news sites. The Graduate School of Journalism at the University of California Berkeley was an early adopter of the use of blogs, in 2002.[42]

As Jim Brady, the executive editor of *The Washington Post*'s site, put it, "Despite the skepticism many still harbor about blogs, there's no denying the impact they've made on society. The rise of easy-to-use blogging software has put a printing press in the hand of every citizen . . . the days of the one-way conversation are over; we now know we need to engage the people consuming our products."[43]

In this kind of environment, some felt the need for a code of ethics, just for news bloggers. *The Spokesman-Review*, in Washington state, developed one of its own. The paper had been a pioneer in other ways, including adopting the SPJ ethics code for its staff and reader-sponsored blogs, some 40 strong, in 2006. Using outside help from the American Press Institute and Poynter, a two-day, media-ethics workshop yielded some blog-specific guidelines, including guidance on who owned what content, with space for follow-on drafting and review. That included guidance—some of it not binding, about when and how to use photos.[44]

One independent journalist, Chris Nolan, described her work for Spot-on.com as "stand-alone . . . not affiliated with any one news association," and who used "time-tested editorial metrics to do [her] job to produce professional, quality editorial [material]."[45] Nolan, who had worked in more traditional newsrooms, including *The San Jose Mercury News* and *The New York Post*, ran what was essentially a distributed newsroom, a shared blog focused on politics and news relevant to nonprofits, and with a staff of nine.

As she described her work, "The blog is simply a tool; it's a piece of software that allows you to write and publish on the Web. It's not so different from what goes on in newsrooms. We're able to research stories on the Web, write them and e-mail them to others."[46]

When approached by Nick Denton, the founder of Gawker Media, to start a news blog in 2001, she pursued the chance to do journalism online via blogging platforms, including web sites that made use of Movable Type, before founding Spot-on.com as a kind of syndication service. Nolan was enthusiastic about news online, especially original reporting and commentary supported by readers. She distinguished her effort from that of more overtly political bloggers, such as Markos Moulitsas, of Daily Kos, and Josh Marshall, of Talking Points Memo, both of which leaned politically left, and Redstate, which leaned right. Nolan believed journalist-driven blogging was a positive force for getting more news online. "The news business made a lot of mistakes, and a lot of that is because they did not have a competitive environment in which to work," she said. "Blogs are a new competitive environment, and that's great because the competition makes us all better."[47]

She identified many mainstream newspaper sites as not attractive and hard to engage with, with some exemptions, including magazines such as *Vanity Fair*. Her advice was to think more agnostically about particular platforms or tools: "When you place emphasis on technology, the message gets lost. . . . Don't spend a lot of time mastering [a] specific technology because it will continue to change. The emphasis must be on basic reporting and writing," which had become a common refrain by the late 2000s.[48]

Still, one could get the sense that journalists did not quite know what to do with blogs through the end of the decade, with explainer pieces reiterating basics (although one could argue that this just meant that they increased in popularity as actual tools, instead of mere curiosities). Use of Really Simple Syndication (RSS) and more sophisticated deployment of search tools, including search tools that searched other search engines, such as Dogpile.com, as well as Zuula.com, which searched blog content from up to nine blogging platforms, showed a maturing interest in the use of the web for journalism. It was easier to collaborate via Google Docs, track news via Google Alerts, build polls via sites like Blogpoll.com or Bravenet.com, surveys via Survey Monkey, (basic) text translations via AltaVista's Babel Fish, FreeTranslation.com, and Google Translate, edit photos via Picasa, Picnik.com or Pixer.us, host them via Flickr.com or Shutterfly.com, edit short movies with iMovie or Windows Movie Maker, or audio with Audacity, or make slideshows with Soundslides. All of these tools and more—at this point in the late 2000s Google was busy acquiring many of them, even if it would jettison a number in time—could all be hosted on specialized blogging platforms run by Blogger.com, LiveJournal.com or WordPress.com. These represented "aspects of Web 2.0" technologies that collectively supercharged the ability of even entry-level journalists to do journalism online.[49]

As Megan Sapnar Ankerson has explored in her book, *Dot-com Design*, this was an outgrowth of previous efforts to make the web easier to use, for both professionals and amateurs alike.[50] Journalists, or at least some of their managers, were eager to enlist the free or low-cost contributions of the latter via the "citizen journalist" movement, including CNN, with its I-Reporters, and the Associated Press, with NowPublic.com, which the AP claimed was "the world's largest participatory news network with more than 60,000 contributors from 140 countries," supplementing its 4,000-strong staff.[51]

Still, toward the end of the decade, legitimate criticisms of blogging-as-journalism remained. Detractors pointed out, correctly, that only a small fraction of blogs did their own reporting (one study put that number as low as five percent of all blogs). Despite the hype about their influence, they would not exist without the hard work of journalists. But, arguably, along with the mobile journalism they helped to enable, they came to symbolize the difference between the darkest depths of what went wrong with moving journalism more online, and some of the brightest possibilities of what could go right with that same process—simultaneously. Blogs *did*, at least for a time, serve as an important bridge between early social media as we have come to know it and the hard work of tough-to-pay-for original reporting. Done well, they helped fill an information vacuum, and if done by journalists, they could expand storytelling in interesting ways.[52]

Of course, the challenging part *was* getting paid, and few bloggers made enough to have that be their primary job. "In short, it's a Wild West out there for bloggers—even though, without them, the Internet's frontier would not have expanded so broadly or so rapidly," noted one blogger-journalist, in 2008. Echoing older advocates for new kinds of media workers in ages past, bloggers wanted to get paid, though their range and level of investment varied wildly, from those who did it purely for enjoyment and those who wanted to make a living from it. That latter group included people who thought it was time to organize online writers, an idea that would eventually, come to pass and is an ongoing movement.[53] By the end of 2008, there were an estimated 70 million blogs.[54]

Mobile reporting with the internet, via blogs

The internet enabled a new generation of reporters to report from the field. The "portable" journalism of the mid-century set the stage for the "mobile" journalism of the last decade of that same century, and the first decade of the new one.[55] As Rachel Plotnick and Meryl Alper have discussed, older ideas of portability foreshadowed many of the basic tenets of mobile journalism.[56] Mobility, as previous generations of journalists learned, did not necessarily bring more independence and less work.

Quite the opposite was true, with reporters, in many less-than-ideal circumstances, being asked to "do more with less" and with corporate ownership not keen on the time and money it took to train a reporter well in a new technology tool. Historically, journalists have engaged in a complex negotiation with the actual control and independence they have over their work, when not done physically in the newsroom.[57]

Sometimes referred to as "backpack journalism," newspapers large and small dabbled with equipping a reporter with a laptop, digital camera, recorder, microphones, a smartphone and other devices in order to have them capture news either exclusively for, or often aimed at, new sites. From Rochester, New York at the *Democrat & Chronicle* to Portland at *The Oregonian*, newspapers experimented with sending a handful of their reporters out in this manner—or tried out teams and attempted to rotate their staffs so they could have a chance to try out the technology.[58]

Sometimes Wi-Fi emitters would be sent out too, if a reporter could not access a hotspot to write up their story and send in their photos, video or audio.[59] One columnist compared it to the kinds of work that wire-service reporters did earlier in the century, rushing to the phones to call in a scoop or a longer piece. He highlighted how the *Orlando Sentinel*, *The Chicago Tribune* and Bloomberg News were places where this shift was occurring, with the need for print reporters to think more like broadcast reporters. "The good news: you'll still need to be able to write, still need to know how to explain things simply, still need to know a good picture and still need to understand what's important and what's not. Pretty much everything else is up for grabs, though."[60]

Mobile phones, with their Short Message Service (SMS) capacity, previewed the capacity of these devices to both send and read the news, paving the way for the iPhone and Android phones that became ubiquitous in the 2010s.[61] Echoing early radio cars, some newsrooms (even some very small ones) equipped SUVs with enough gear to help them serve as a "mobile news delivery station." That is what happened with a small news site based in Fort Bend County, Texas. Reporters had access to "a Palm Pilot device that combines telephone and e-mail, and uses Bluetooth technology to provide Internet access to the reporters' laptops, wherever they may be."[62]

Efforts such as these blurred the old lines that had been drawn out of necessity between reporters, photographs and videographers, combining the roles, perhaps at the expense of one of those skillsets.[63] Some reporters assigned to “mojo” (mobile journalism) work worried about the workload, including at *The Atlanta Journal-Constitution*. Bert Roughton Jr., who was the managing editor of the print version of the paper, noted that “if you were to break this down into a factory, I think we’re being called upon to produce more product, and we do have fewer people . . . some reporters who feel that they’re running as hard as they can and it’s not quite hard enough.” The paper had gone down to 430 staffers from more than 500, and had to cut its coverage of national and international news.[64]

Nonetheless, some gifted reporters, whether by training and good luck, or both, could get decent at the various skillsets now required of them. Jennifer Brett, a reporter in the paper’s “News & Information and Enterprise” department, tasked with working for the blogging side, believed that “a lot of newspapers are writing the Book of Revelation. You know, ‘These are the end times.’ It’s almost like we’re writing the Book of Genesis.”[65]

John Strauss, who worked for *The Indianapolis Star* as a multimedia reporter, recounted how he covered the Indiana State Fair as a “backpack journalist” in 2003, complete with a “Mac Book laptop, Canon 53 IS digital camera, sound recorder, tripod and other gear.” Strauss, who had experience working for the AP, was no stranger to working at a frantic pace, and he had been sent by his paper as a kind of experiment, with the goal to “to write for online and print, shoot photos and edit TV-style video packages, all in the same news cycle.”[66]

Strauss had support from the paper’s web designers, who constructed a separate page for him, and in 10 days he ultimately wrote 32 updates to his professional blog, writing more than 10,000 words in the process, and taking 26 photos and five videos “about fair food, harness horses, 4-H kids, the near-record hot weather and the Midway rides.” The blog posts were repurposed for the daily print newspaper, and the photos were used for the blog posts, with the video reused for other stories. Strauss covered some breaking news along the way, when some 100 people had to be treated for temperature-related injuries on the fair’s first day.[67]

Strauss said that his readers “loved it, judging from the high number of page views, e-mail responses and encounters at the-fairgrounds.” But he felt it was not a realistic test for most of his colleagues, due to having had some experience in TV, with his AP background and because he already wrote for his home paper’s site. He worked 12-hour days, and confessed that he could have used another person there to support him, given the difficulties in balancing all the tasks he had to complete.[68]

Other newspapers, such as *The News-Press* in Fort Myers, Florida, went even further, blending video and print reporting. According to the paper’s digital editor, Mark Bickel, the paper had grown from having five dedicated mobile journalists to pushing all its reporting staff to think of themselves in that role. "What we have figured out is that people are going to click on the car accident, the fire, breaking news. That's what drives traffic to the Web site."[69]

The Long Island, New York-based *Newsday* was trying something similar, training half of its newsroom staff to shoot video, despite some reluctance. Jonathan McCarthy, who was the assistant managing editor, said that a largely self-selected group emerged: "They're gung-ho about it. While it was a struggle three or four years ago to get people to file for the Web, we're past that now." He noted that younger, recent graduates of journalism programs tended to be more comfortable with technology and training for it.[70]

The acquisition has employees at all four newspapers excited. "I think the general consensus is, 'Thank God we've finally been purchased by a newspaper company,'" said Rich Hood, vice president and editorial page editor of the *Kansas City Star*.

—J.C.

The Fourth Estate

By Steve Greenberg

4 Editor & Publisher ■ April 12, 1997

Figure 5.1 "The Fourth Estate."

Source: "The Fourth Estate," *Editor & Publisher*, April 12, 1997, 4

Randy Covington, who helped to run the Ifra Newsplex's Training Center, a "newsroom of the future" based at the University of South Carolina, observed that newspapers were still mostly experimenting with blending different kinds of media content on their sites, but acknowledged that concerns about the future of the industry—especially on the business side—made some news workers anxious about learning new tools. What was important was focus, and the right training for these workers.[71]

"News organizations will be best served if they focus on stories. How can I tell this story the best way? Is this a story that might lend itself to audio, to a slideshow? Is this a story where you really need to have video?" He highlighted the *Rocky Mountain News* and the *Detroit Free Press* with their efforts, toward that end.[72]

There remained a role for print- and text-based storytelling, but multimedia reporting was not going away: "I don't think anybody can stick their head in the sand and say this is a passing trend. . . . This is a reality. You either do it, or we risk not having jobs."[73] That sense of all-or-nothing investment was not isolated to Atlanta. By the end of the decade, many news workers really felt that their choices with technology were narrowing, the stakes for success or failure growing, and that the internet was less an open-ended platform of possibilities and much more of a necessity for day-to-day news work.

Conclusion

Beginning with blogs and concerns over the place of user-generated content, to an increased focus on mobile journalism, the 2000s saw a major shift in *how* journalism was conducted online, and how news workers felt about it. With that came increased trepidation about future developments in the journalism industry. That happened as social-media platforms like Twitter became popular, and the white-hot enthusiasm for blogging mellowed out, perhaps with some of that zeal switching over to podcasting.

Twitter, which launched in 2006, was initially thought of as more akin to the "unassuming police scanner sitting on your desk" by at least one observer in 2008, instead of the journalist-centric microblogging tool it turned out to be.[74] It was hard to predict—perhaps impossible—that tools like it would, in time, supplant the blog in popularity, and, arguably, power, though the resiliency of news-blogs should not be understated.

In any event, when thinking about how the internet impacted newsrooms in the 2000s, as opposed to the 1990s, it is easier to see the concrete ways it changed journalism, with pressure on reporters to update throughout the day, and to engage more with their various publics, via blogging platforms.

These platforms shifted power to some readers and to a number of dedicated bloggers, but they did not undo the need for reporting.

As the media-industry observers in this chapter noted, reporters had busily filed updates to their stories in the days before the internet—doing so via the latter was not necessarily new. What *was* new was how some of these tools had eroded the industry's advertising-driven business model. That would push the field to the brink and beyond in terms of how to pay for journalism. Outside of big national brands, local and regional papers would continue to struggle with their transitions online.

What happened by the end of the 2000s is the subject of the next and final chapter.

Notes

1 Alan Rusbridger, *Breaking News: The Remaking of Journalism and Why It Matters Now* (New York: Picador, 2017).
2 Andrew Perrin and Maeve Duggan, "Americans' Internet Access: 2000–2015," *Pew Research Center*, June 26, 2015, accessed September 11, 2021, www.pewresearch.org/internet/2015/06/26/americans-internet-access-2000-2015/.
3 Staff Report, "Household Internet Use Survey," *The Daily*, Statistics Canada, July 26, 2001, accessed September 11, 2001, https://www150.statcan.gc.ca/n1/daily-quotidien/010726/dq010726a-eng.htm; Staff Report, "Canadian Internet Use Survey," Statistics Canada, January 1, 2013, accessed September 11, 2021, https://www150.statcan.gc.ca/n1/daily-quotidien/110525/dq110525b-eng.htm.
4 William H. Dutton and Ellen J. Heisper, "The Internet in Britain," *Oxford Internet Survey, Oxford Internet Institute*, 2007, accessed September 11, 2021, https://oxis.oii.ox.ac.uk/wp-content/uploads/sites/43/2014/11/oxis2007-report.pdf; William H. Dutton and Grant Blank, "Next Generation Users: The Internet in Britain," *Oxford Internet Survey, Oxford Internet Institute*, 2011, accessed September 11, 2021, http://blogs.oii.ox.ac.uk/oxis/wp-content/uploads/sites/43/2014/11/oxis2011-report.pdf.
5 David Karpf, "Something I No Longer Believe: Is Internet Time Slowing Down?" *Social Media + Society*, July–September 2019, 1–4, https://journals.sagepub.com/doi/pdf/10.1177/2056305119849492.
6 As a reminder, this project is not meant to be an exhaustive media history of all things related to the internet and the journalism industry, but a focused study looking at some key themes and narratives.
7 Stuart Allan, *Online News: Journalism and the Internet* (Berkshire, UK: Open University Press, 2005), 58.
8 Bill Mitchell, "How 9/11 Changed Poynter (and Journalism)," *Poynter.org*, September 9, 2021, accessed September 9, 2021, www.poynter.org/reporting-editing/2021/how-9-11-changed-poynter-and-journalism/; see also Mike Wendland, "Overloaded Internet Fails Info-Starved Americans," *Detroit Free Press*, September 11, 2001, accessed September 12, 2001, http://web.archive.org/web/20020611064222/www.poynter.org/Terrorism/Mike1.htm.
9 Allan, *Online News*, 60–62, 63.
10 Ibid., 64–65.

11 Ibid., 68; see also Lee Rainie, "How Americans Used the Internet After the Terror Attack," *Pew Internet & American Life Project*, September 15, 2001, accessed September 12, 2001, https://webarchive.loc.gov/all/20011008224148/www.pewinternet.org/reports/pdfs/pip_terror_report.pdf.
12 Allan, *Online News*, 69; see also Steve Outing, "The First Shock of History," *Poynter.org*, November 5, 2001.
13 Allan, *Online News*, 69, 70–71; for more on the transition to a more "digital first," i.e., web-based journalism at the start of the 2000s, see John Pavlik, *Journalism and New Media* (New York: Columbia University Press, 2001).
14 Allan, *Online News*, 74.
15 David Porter, *Internet Culture* (New York: Routledge, 1997), xvii. Porter made this observation in his introduction to a collection of 15 essays by such scholars as Michele Tepper, Mizuko Ito, James Knapp and Shannon McRae.
16 Brian McCullough, *How the Internet Happened: From Netscape to the iPhone* (New York: W.W. Norton & Co., 2018), 237.
17 Ibid., 243.
18 Politico Staff, "BIRTHDAY OF THE DAY: Brian Stelter, Host of CNN's 'Reliable Sources' and Senior Media Correspondent," *Politico*, September 3, 2018, accessed September 12, 2021, www.politico.com/story/2018/09/03/playbook-birthday-brian-stelter-806293.
19 Another example of a blogger who essentially blogged their way into mainstreamed journalism during this post-9/11 era is Glenn Reynolds, "a law professor with a technological bent," as well as a contrarian, libertarian perspective, who started Instapundit.com a few weeks before 9/11. See Dan Gillmor, *We the Media: Grassroots Journalism by the People, for the People* (Sebastopol, CA: O'Reilly, 2004), 21–22. Gillmor expands more on the ideas in *We the Media* in his 2010 book, *Mediactive*, which he self-published.
20 Gillmor, *We the Media*, 22.
21 J. D. Lasica, "Taking Ethics to the Net: Despite Some Controversies, Online Journalists Have Done a Good Job of Sticking to Traditional Values," *Quill*, July–August 2001, 42–45. "Prediction: The decade ahead promises to thrust online newsgathering techniques into the spotlight far more prominently as untold thousands of Net users take on the mantle of amateur reporters and begin lone-wolf operations to cover stories in their back yards and neighborhoods, complete with Weblogs and video footage online but absent the standards of professional newsrooms. Stay tuned."
22 Matt Welch, "Blogworld and Its Gravity: The New Amateur Journalists Weigh in," *Columbia Journalism Review*, September–October 2003, 21–26.
23 Tim Rutten, "Riordan's Fourth Estate Sending Prototype to Press," *Los Angeles Times*, January 22, 2003, accessed September 13, 2021, www.latimes.com/archives/la-xpm-2003-jan-22-et-rutten22-story.html; Welch, "Blogworld and Its Gravity," 21–26.
24 Welch, "Blogworld and Its Gravity," 21–26.
25 "Pyra labs . . . had a revolutionary insight that made all this popular: every technological requirement of Web publishing—graphic design, simple coding for things like links, hosting—is a barrier to entry, keeping non-techies out; why not remove them?" He also lists a number of individuals as being either key bloggers or programmers or both: Evan Williams, Paul Bausch, Meg Hourihan, Rebecca Blood, Jason Kottke, Joshua Micah Marshall, Mickey Kaus, Andrew Sullivan and Virginia Postrel.

26 Welch, "Blogworld and Its Gravity," 21–26.
27 Ibid; see also Matt Welch, "The Media Go Blogging," *Columbia Journalism Review*, September–October 2003, 23.
28 Jay Rosen, "Terms of Authority: Readers and Viewers—Rich Now in Alternative Sources of News—Are More Assertive and Far Less in Awe of the Press," *Columbia Journalism Review*, September–October 2003, 35–37.
29 Jesse Oxfeld, "Blogs Rolling in 2005: With Web Logs All the Rage, Newspapers Try to Cash in on the Trend. Some Sites Are Even Getting Overhauls to Make Them More Blogger-Friendly," *Editor & Publisher*, January 2005, 36–40. This researcher participated in a similar effort, on a far smaller scale, in 2004, with *The Seattle Times*, contributing to a blog that covered local, state and national politics.
30 Jesse Oxfeld, "Letting the Blogs Out: Why a Daily in Greensboro, N.C., Decided to Get a Little Radical and Create an Online 'Town Square'," *Editor & Publisher*, March 2005, 38–40, 42.
31 Greg Mitchell, "Dangling 'Conversation'? When Bloggers Hit Too Close to Home: New Conflicts and Controversies Arise as Newspapers Almost Everywhere Embrace Web Logs," *Editor & Publisher*, January 2006, 20.
32 Joe Strupp, "Mixing, Matching, and Multimedia: With Merged Newsrooms and Continuous Coverage, the Web/Print Hybrid Is Becoming a Reality. In Part I of a Series, We Look at Its Requirements—and Rewards," *Editor & Publisher*, March 2006, 64–68.
33 Dave Astor, "Online and Ongoing: The Blogging Life, Huffington-Style: Arianna Huffington Discusses *The Huffington Post* as the Popular Group/News Site Approaches Its First Birthday," *Editor & Publisher*, April 2006, 76, 78. See Michael Shapiro, "Six Degrees of Aggregation: How the Huffington Post Ate the Internet," *Columbia Journalism Review*, June 2012, accessed August 1, 2021, https://archives.cjr.org/cover_story/six_degrees_of_aggregation.php.
34 Miki Johnson, "Denver's 'Hub' Goes National: This Local Experiment in Citizen Journalism Can Now Be Adapted Everywhere," *Editor & Publisher*, May 2006, 12–13.
35 Joe Strupp, "2008 Campaign Special: No Longer on the Fringe, Political Bloggers Now Drive Coverage," *Editor & Publisher*, December 2007, 22–26, 28; see also Christopher J. Feola, "Newspapers Gain with Technology: On-line's Inexpensive Outlays Give Journalists Other Opportunities to Advance Talent," *Quill*, April 1996, 27–29.
36 Maria Trombly, "Looking for Online Dollars: News Providers Are Finding Ways to Make Their Web Sites Profitable," *Quill*, May 2002, 18–21. In this case, a blog was defined (yet again) for readers, as an "online Web log or diary."
37 Renée Petrina, "Session Avoids Getting 'Blogged' Down When Addressing Latest Internet Craze," *Quill*, October–November 2004, 15.
38 Patrick Beeson, "Blogging: What Is It? And How Has It Affected the Media?" *Quill*, March 2005, 16–19.
39 Ibid. Blood also defined a blog as "a Web site with a continuous, chronological series of posts—some inviting comments from readers—on any topic imaginable, often containing links to sites throughout the Internet." It is interesting to note these evolving definitions, over time. "Blood is a blogging elder of sorts—her posts date to April 1999, the early days of blogs. Her status has given her a unique perspective on how the medium evolved from a small group of Web designers linking to interesting or unique Web sites, to outlets influencing the

journalistic record. But the reason blogs became funneled into the mainstream instead of being confined in eddies of the Internet is almost as important as their impact." See also Mallory Jensen, "A Brief History of Weblogs," *Columbia Journalism Review*, September–October 2003, accessed September 12, 2021, https://go.gale.com/ps/i.do?id=GALE%7CA109264376&sid=googleScholar&v=2.1&it=r&linkaccess=abs&issn=0010194X&p=AONE&sw=w&userGroupName=anon%7Eb8b61179.

40 Beeson, "Blogging," 16–19.

41 Ibid. Though eventually shut down after an attempt at unionization by its staff (see Anna Heyward, "The Story Behind the Unjust Shutdown of Gothamist and DNAinfo," *The New Yorker*, November 14, 2017, accessed September 12, 2021, www.newyorker.com/culture/culture-desk/the-story-behind-the-unjust-shutdown-of-gothamist-and-dnainfo), they live on (Andy Newman, "Gothamist Will Publish Again in Deal with WNYC," *The New York Times*, February 23, 2018, accessed September 12, 2021, www.nytimes.com/2018/02/23/nyregion/gothamist-dnainfo-deal-wnyc-publish-again.html).

42 Patrick Beeson, "Bringing Blogs into the Classroom: 'New Media' Platform Gaining Steam at Universities," *Quill*, August 2005, 27–29; for a surviving example, see http://rimrats.blogspot.com/, from the University of Arizona. Blogs seemed to have been a popular way to teach opinion writing, although this researcher took an advanced reporting class in which he was required to do original reporting via a basic blog. He shares the URL here, though he is a bit embarrassed to do so: https://willmari.wordpress.com/about/.

43 Jim Brady, "High Velocity Journalism: Inside Washingtonpost.com Where the Web Has Created a New Generation of Online Journalists Working Around the Clock," *The Journalist* (published by *Quill*), October–November 2005, 64–67.

44 "Newspaper Works to Include Blogging in Code of Ethics," *Quill*, December 2006, 27.

45 Wendy Hoke, "Chris Nolan: Quill Poses 10 Questions to People with Some of the Coolest Jobs in Journalism," *Quill*, January–February 2007, 18–19; From its "About Us" page: "Spot-On Takes Cutting Edge Silicon Valley Technology and Applies It to the Political, Advocacy and Nonprofit Arenas," accessed September 13, 2021, https://spot-on.com/about.

46 Hoke, "Chris Nolan," 18–19.

47 Ibid; "For an industry of people who thrive on delivering the message of change, we don't embrace it well ourselves. I think a lot of people have faith in the business and how it will go forward. Others are not able to envision the future, and that's gut-wrenching. Either way, it's time for the whining to come down to a dull roar."

48 Hoke, "Chris Nolan," 18–19.

49 Jeff Smith, "The Web's Hidden Gems: Technology Often Means Steep Prices, Steep Learning or Both. But a Number of Recent Innovations Are Free and Easy to Use, and They Offer Tremendous Benefits for Journalists, Journalism Educators and Journalism Students," *Quill*, August 2007, 27–31. See also Anonymous Staff Writer, "Zuula Unveils Powerful New Internet Search Service," *PRWeb.com*, accessed September 13, 2021, www.prweb.com/releases/2006/12/prweb490162.htm.

50 Megan Sapnar Ankerson, *Dot-Com Design: The Rise of a Usable, Social, Commercial Web* (New York: New York University Press, 2018).

51 Smith, "The Web's Hidden Gems," 27–31.

52 Robert Kuttner, "The Race: Newspapers Can Make It to a Bright Print-Digital Future After All—But Only If They Run Fast and Dodge Wall Street," *Columbia Journalism Review*, March–April 2007, 24–32; Kuttner argued for a kind of middle-grade blog, the "Carefully-Researched Weblogs," or "crog," that served an important information-filling role in an information society; see also Pew staff, "The State of the News Media 2006," *Pew*, March 13, 2006, accessed September 13, 2021, www.pewtrusts.org/en/research-and-analysis/reports/2006/03/13/the-state-of-the-news-media-2006.

53 Chris Mooney, "Blogonomics: Bloggers of the World, Unite!" *Columbia Journalism Review*, January–February 2008, 18–19; "Individual blogs, and Web sites hosting large numbers of bloggers, are profiting—not just culturally and intellectually, but economically—from bloggers' work. Organizing, in that sense, seems not only inevitable but necessary; 'professional' bloggers need to be compensated for their work."; Will Mari, "Writer by Trade: James Ralph's Claims to Authorship," *Authorship* 4, no. 2 (2015): 1–17; see also the work of Errol Salamon.

54 Bree Nordenson, "Overload! Journalism's Battle for Relevance in an Age of Too Much Information," *Columbia Journalism Review*, November–December 2008, 30–32, 35–37, 40, 42.

55 Will Mari, "Technology in the Newsroom: Adoption of the Telephone and the Radio Car from c. 1920 to 1960," *Journalism Studies* 19, no. 9 (2018): 1366–89.

56 Rachel Plotnick, "Tethered Women, Mobile Men: Gendered Mobilities of Typewriting," *Mobile Media & Communication* 8, no. 2 (May 2020): 188–208; Meryl Alper, "Portables, Luggables, and Transportables: Historicizing the Imagined Affordances of Mobile Computing," *Mobile Media & Communication* 7, no. 3 (September 2019): 322–40.

57 Henrik Örnebring and Amy Schmitz Weiss, "Journalism and the Politics of Mobility," *Journalism Studies* (published online, 2001).

58 Joe Strupp, "Going Mobile: Facing Deadline—and Multimedia—Demands, Reporters Make Streets and Coffeeshops the New Office," *Editor & Publisher*, May 2008, 24–28, 30.

59 Art Home, "Shoptalk: Mobile: The Future? Why Newspapers Must Prepare to Go Wireless, and Quickly," *Editor & Publisher*, June 2008, 70.

60 David Cole, "Back to the Future: As Technology Expands, the Daily Reporter's Routine Might Resemble That of the Old-Time Wire Service Journalist," *Quill*, March 2000, 13–15.

61 Rob Curley, "It's About the News, Not the Paper: Seven Basic Steps News Organizations Should Take to Ensure Success in Today's Tech Climate," *The Journalist* (published by *Quill*), October–November 2007, 23–25.

62 Bob Dunn, "Backpack Journalism: Taking Web News to Its Logical Extreme," *Quill*, March 2008, 20–21.

63 Julia M. Klein, "If You Build It. . . : The 'Journal-Constitution' Gambles on a Digitally Driven Makeover," *Columbia Journalism Review*, November–December 2007, 40–45.

64 Ibid.

65 Ibid.

66 John Strauss, "Backpack Journalism: Print and Online: The Balancing Act," *Quill*, March 2008, 18–19.

67 Ibid.

68 Ibid.

69 Ibid.
70 Ibid.
71 Ibid.
72 Ibid.
73 Ibid.
74 Nicole Garrison-Sprenger, "Twittery-do-dah, Twittering Pays," *Quill*, October–November 2008, 12–15; Brandon Griggs and Heather Kelly, "23 Key Moments from Twitter History," *CNN*, September 16, 2013, accessed September 13, 2021, www.cnn.com/2013/09/13/tech/social-media/twitter-key-moments/index.html.

6 Conclusion

The internet disrupted journalism . . . but what next?

When reflecting on the many ways the suite of technologies encompassed by the internet impacted the newspaper industry in North America and the UK, the paths taken and those-not-taken show the futility of easy stories about the still-ongoing transition from an analog to a digital news ecosystem. Journalism continues to have a troubled relationship with technology tools, looking to them as saviors, or enemies, but not really something in between. News workers have often resisted change, worried about their jobs, and this was the case with the computerization of the newsroom. Ultimately, reporters and editors largely kept the heart of their routines intact through the pre-internet era.[1]

But both the felt pace of change and the actual pace of changes increased in the latter half of the 1990s, especially as news sites became mainstream. Later, in the 2000s, as Web 2.0 technologies increased both interactivity *and* the ability of non-journalists to, if not directly compete with, but at least challenge, news organizations, that pace began to feel dizzying, almost disorienting, especially when combined with financial challenges.[2]

Readers and news workers alike were feeling overwhelmed with the proliferation of options and technology tools by the end of the decade, contributing to a sense of information fatigue.[3] "Add to this mix the seemingly endless variety of blogs, and it's no wonder that many readers—even professional journalists—feel lost," noted one writer. But in the midst of tumultuous, even disastrous, change, journalists felt like they could then (and may still) serve today as a guide through the chaos, even if that environment has gotten far more competitive since the late 2000s.[4]

Disruption and media history

As journalism studies scholars have pointed out, applying the theory of disruptive innovation to newsrooms must fight simplistic stereotypes, including presumptions about the kinds of newsrooms (usually wealthier)

DOI: 10.4324/9780429324871-6

able to handle and enact change. Instead, many newsrooms had to face the "liability of newness, which principally contends that faced with disruptive technology, even old organizations have to essentially become new organizations." By focusing on "core competencies," organizations can and do survive severe and sudden changes, and at its best, data journalism, mobile journalism and open-source tools—all emerging out of the industry's earlier encounters with change, in the 1990s and before—show promise for the future. But more needs to be done for smaller news organizations in the US, Canada and UK if those kinds of changes can make their way down to less-financially secure organizations.[5]

In other words, online news needs to be delivered effectively and sustainably not just by the *Guardians* of the world but also by the *Slough Observer*, and not only by *The Seattle Times* but also by *The Snoqualmie Valley Record*. How, exactly, that could and may yet happen is outside the scope of this short book, but the history of these efforts certainly informs the present in real ways.

Media history provides a helpful, centered lens through which to view the many and myriad changes of the past 30 years. As Boczkowski has argued, "the heuristic value of a historical perspective in the study of emerging media" is helpful when looking at the "dynamics of this culture of innovation."[6] Media history "helps to avoid some misunderstandings about the efforts by American dailies in the area of consumer-oriented alternatives to print," especially the idea "that the creation and growth of online newspapers on the web was some sort of revolutionary occurrence and without any roots in the past."[7]

Following this call to *avoid* a breathless pronouncement that the internet upturned all things all at once, this study has shown that, in fact, the journalism industry reacted to the internet in ways both rational—through joint efforts such as the New Century Network and funding devoted to research—and irrational, including the slow response to the threat posed by online-ad-oriented start-ups such as Craigslist, and in the long hesitancy about what to do with such tools as blogs or mobile reporting.

But it has *also*, this author hopes, shown the complexities, and even the chaos, of certain moments, such as the late 1990s and the worry about the use of even-then limited resources to develop "original content," and the long, not easily dismissed, concern about the consequences of charging for that online content, when only specialist publications generally succeeded in doing so. Cultural contexts also matter, and have only comparatively recently been investigated by scholars, when it comes to how technology adoption works in non-US contexts.[8]

Only by appreciating the fluidity of these moments, and the path-dependent turns that came out of them, often *not* by intention, can we see how the pivot to online news was not as fated to be *as* fraught as we have come to believe. It would be smug of us to think that patterns in the near past are easy to see. As Boczkowski has pointed out, we should appreciate just how much innovation happened, and how much *did* change, in a comparatively short amount of time, demonstrating the flexibility and resiliency of journalism as a field.[9] Of course, how to pay for it remains an open question.

But the generation that saw the computerization of the newsroom from the 1960s through the 1990s, and the generation after, that saw first-hand the Internetization of those same spaces—yes, sometimes with dilatory impacts on the needed numbers of news workers—were impressive in their capacity to not just absorb change, but lean into it. This was the case despite the mistakes and misdirections that are usually the focus of research on journalism's digital existence.

Imagining futures that could-have-been and are

Both Knight Ridder and the *Columbia Journalism Review* spent time and resources forecasting possible paths for the news industry. In both cases, they involved a certain amount of educated guesswork, but the thinking underlying their predictions is worth considering here, briefly.

The latter was a serious attempt to think through various impacts on the paper's bottom line, especially due to what Knight Ridder called "economic factors," "demographic forces/change," "sociological/educational developments," "technology-driven developments," "competition" and "potential newspaper actions," or, rather, responses. The technology-driven developments tried to factor in changes in "electronic classified," i.e., online ads, the growth of video, including new forms of interactive TV, but also new "flat-panel" devices, desktop publishing, fax or other remote ways of accessing the news, but also what was broadly conceived as "tailored newspaper production" and the "digitization of information," anticipating the concept of the "daily me," as popularized by Nicholas Negroponte, the director of MIT's Media Lab in the 1990s, and his students.[10]

Among possible reactions by the industry (really, by Knight Ridder) were a more aggressive move into online ads, "potential alliances with telcos" [telecommunication companies], cable, etc." and more targeted marketing and promotion. But the chief concern was what would happen to an aging reader base, "contraction of reading time," growing illiteracy and the problem of younger readers simply not picking up physical papers as much as previous transitionary generations had. A major threat was not so much the internet, per se, but cable companies and their ability to create more local content that could cut into the comfortably profitable base of newspapers.

The first possible future, "Scenario Alpha" was "presented in the form of an interview of a senior Knight-Ridder executive by a writer working on a history of the newspaper business during the 1990s." The second, "Scenario Beta," was imagined as "an excerpt from a management presentation in 2003 to a Special Board Committee . . . in the year 2012." The final, darkest future was "Scenario Gamma," which was "in the form of an off-the-record interview of a former Knight-Ridder executive by a writer working on a history of the newspaper business during the 1990s."

High-speed, optical-fiber delivered internet, "video-on-demand and virtual paper," with "electronic delivery via television and computers" was broadly anticipated, but the web was not, per se. The Alpha scenario, subtitled, "the most likely outcome," showed some modest losses and some retrenchment in the face of new technologies, but also still-strong growth, with more than $1 billion in advertising revenue generated over 20 years, even with profit growth down from nearly 20 percent annually to closer to 6 or 7 percent. The Beta scenario was the most optimistic, showing nearly 12 percent profit through 2002, and nearly four billion in total revenue. "Augmentation," which included robust investment in new technology platforms and key alliances that ultimately did not come to pass (see, for example, the fate of the NCN), was cited as key to this particularly happy future. The final, Gamma, scenario was grimmer. Labeled, "serious deterioration," it predicted a major decrease in readership, as well as an increase in newsprint costs (a concern in all the scenarios), but also sluggish growth in advertising revenue, so much so that annual growth fell to 3.2 percent. This was due to a faster-than-expected move to video and the "electronic delivery of information, led by the telcos," and a lack of investment in new-media technologies. But, reassured the report, "at this point in 1992, our newspaper business is strong. Profit margins are the envy of most industries. Cash flow is strong. Our balance sheet is solid. And we are clearly set to benefit from a rebound in the economy."[11]

By 2004, Knight Ridder was a more sober company, having experienced not quite the dire forecasting of its 1992 Gamma scenario, but neither its optimistic Beta scenario. The company met to consider what had actually occurred and what to do about it. As Jerry Ceppos, the vice president for news at the time, put it, in his summary, "we need to do a better job [to] competitively position our newspapers against other media with respect to providing perspective on the news."[12] Among the more interesting what-ifs of this moment remains: if Knight Ridder and other companies had more urgently pushed the devices, payment methods and software forward as they *could* have, would they have entered the 2010s as a more robust industry?

In 2009, the *Columbia Journalism Review* took its own turn at prophecy, running in its March/April issue for that year a series of short what-ifs about the future of the field over the next five years. The topics ranged from the fate of a more web-focused *Christian Science Monitor*, NPR's "Planet Money" podcast, how a nonprofit investigative news organization, *The San Francisco Public Press*, could not just survive, but thrive, the role of NGO-funded news, the role of government support in news, and the future profitability of Politico.

But unlike Knight Ridder's prognostications, the continuing, extremely disruptive role of the internet was taken for granted, with a far greater emphasis on nontraditional funding models, especially subscriptions, and with a general return to paywalls.[13]

Why what happened with the internet before, matters now, and may matter later

The stores we tell ourselves about the future reveal truths about the past and present. The same is true with journalism and technology, and about how the internet *might* change things. Usually, the past is not entirely prologue, but it can provide some hints of future trends. Sometimes the best minds in a smart, stable industry can be wrong, or right, but only to a certain degree.

As Knight Ridder found, prophetic analysis does not necessarily yield total doom, but nor does it lead to the best possible future—it often lands somewhere in between. So, it was with the news industry and the internet. There was a 26 percent decline in journalism jobs in the US alone, or from about 114,000 newsroom staff in 2008 to 85,000 in 2020 (with more news and more journalism to do than ever). Despite some promising growth in digital-first outlets, that is still not a good thing for a democratic society, and efforts continue to rectify it, with projects such as Report for America.[14]

Even before this steep decline, the revisiting of paywalls happened throughout the 2000s in the trade press. In 2001, for example, one writer discussed "10 pay-to-play strategies," ranging from strict paywalls, partial paywalls, some targeted, paid-for-niche news via email, so-called "pockets of passion" (targeted content again), collaborations with other sites, such as eBay, convergence efforts, wireless services, reselling content, monetizing archives, and starting an ISP. This was a nuanced conversation and not an all-or-nothing proposition, but a range.[15] Later in the decade, even smaller dailies started to reenact them, as part of an ongoing, not a once-and-done, decision.[16]

One of the dangers—that this project has sought to correct, even if gently—of examining the recent past, including with issues like paywalls in journalism, is to think of that past as somehow preordained. That means that no matter what happened, the journalism industry would have fumbled with the adoption of internet-delivered news, or somehow did worse than it did.

But we must remember that online news was more innovative, more interesting and happening earlier than we tend to give it credit for—and it is possible that our generation will not see so radical a set of changes as our forebears have seen in theirs. To that end, this short history of the internet's arrival in newsrooms has sought to show the contingent ways technology impacts news work. The mutual shaping of humans on technology, and technology on humans, is messy and not susceptible to simple narratives.

The disruption of the internet is no exception.

Notes

1 Will Mari, *A Short History of Disruptive Journalism Technologies: 1960–1990* (Abingdon, UK: Routledge, 2019).

2 A history of the 2008–2009 financial crisis is outside the scope of this book, but scholars such as David Ryfe, Nikki Usher and Victor Packard have conducted excellent ethnographic and survey-driven research about the impacts of that moment on the journalism that came after.

3 Bree Nordenson, "Overload! Journalism's Battle for Relevance in an Age of Too Much Information," *Columbia Journalism Review*, November–December 2008, 30–32, 35–37, 40, 42.

4 Curtis Brainard, "Trimming the Hedges: Web Jungle, Web Garden—You Decide," *Columbia Journalism Review*, November–December 2008, 42. "Since well before the creation of the printing press, there has been more news available on a given day than any one person could follow, and more information than any one reporter could process. It's just that today both reporter and reader have much greater access to the news and information, and as such, there is a greater need to employ filters and other tools to help us organize and manage the deluge."

5 Clayton M. Christensen, *The Innovator's Dilemma: When New Technologies Cause Great Firms to Fail* (Boston, MA: Harvard Business School Press, 1997).

6 Pablo Boczkowski, *Digitizing the News: Innovation in Online Newspapers* (Cambridge, MA: MIT Press, 2005), 49.

7 Ibid., 50.

8 Ruth Moon, "Moto-Taxis, Drivers, Weather, and WhatsApp: Contextualizing New Technology in Rwandan Newsrooms," *Journalism* (published online 2021).

9 Boczkowski, *Digitizing the News*, 51.

10 Knight Ridder Scenario Planning, 1992/2012, April 1992, author's collection; Christopher Harper, "The Daily Me: Customized Online News Services Allow Readers to Receive News Content Tailored to Their Interests. But Do Readers Risk Missing Important Developments That Don't Fit Their Profiles?" *American Journalism Review*, April 1997, accessed September 15, 2021, https://web.archive.org/web/20090328114708/www.ajr.org/Article.asp?id=268; see also Nicholas Negroponte, *Being Digital* (New York: Alfred A. Knopf, 1995).

11 Knight Ridder Scenario Planning, 1992/2012, April 1992, author's collection.

12 Ceppos was reviewing how the various newspapers in the Knight Ridder empire were faring with respect the "Seven Tenets," company-wide principles that included, watchdog, trust, people like me, first & only utility, ease of use

and storytelling. The papers examined included *El Nuevo Herald, The Miami Herald*, the *Philadelphia Daily News, The Detroit Free Press, The Charlotte Observer*, the Wilkes-Barre *Times Leader*, the San Luis Obispo *Tribune, The Kansas City Star, The Akron Beacon Journal, The San Jose Mercury News* and *The Lexington Herald-Leader*, among others. See Knight Ridder Management Conference, "Knight Ridder Journalism: Steady Improvement on the Seven Tenets," March 2004.

13 Carroll Bogart, "Old Hands, New Voice: How NGOs Learned to Do News," *Columbia Journalism Review*, March–April 2009, 29–31; John Yemma, "Unchaining the Monitor: How an Early Web-First Strategy Worked Out," *Columbia Journalism Review*, March–April 2009, 31–32; Adam Davidson, "So Cool: How a Weather Map Changed the Climate," *Columbia Journalism Review*, March–April 2009, 32–34; Michael Stoll and David S. Bennahum, "The New Niche: How Tax Incentives and Technology Came to the Rescue," *Columbia Journalism Review*, March–April 2009, 34–37; Michael Stoll, "No Profit, No Problem: How a New City Daily (on Newsprint!) Rolled," *Columbia Journalism Review*, March–April 2009, 37–38; John F. Harris, "Two Tents: How Politico Might Work Out. Or Not," *Columbia Journalism Review*, March–April 2009, 39–41. For more on nonprofits and journalistic enterprises, see Ruth Moon, "Getting into Living Rooms: NGO Media Relations Work as Strategic Practice," *Journalism* 19, no. 7 (2018): 1011–26.

14 Mason Walker, "U.S. Newsroom Employment Has Fallen 26% Since 2008," *Pew Research Center*, July 13, 2021, accessed September 14, 2021, www.pewresearch.org/fact-tank/2021/07/13/u-s-newsroom-employment-has-fallen-26-since-2008/. See Report for America, www.reportforamerica.org/.

15 Wayne Robins, "No More Free Lunch: More and More Free Web Sites (Finally) Decide They Can't Win If Visitors Don't Pay," *Editor & Publisher*, May 21, 2001, 12–15.

16 Jennifer Saba, "Web Ad Revenue Up Against the Wall," *Editor & Publisher*, April 2008, 14–15; at least 50 were part of an early trend, though they were still in the minority. One paper featured, the *Daily Times* in Waterton, New York, had a fairly expensive $79 a year access charge for its site, or $39 if you had home delivery; the paper had about 1,000 subscribers online. For much more on this topic, see Ángel Arrese, "From Gratis to Paywalls: A Brief History of a Retro-Innovation in the Press's Business," *Journalism Studies* 17, no. 8 (2016): 1051–67. There is a need for future work on this topic, especially as paywalls continue to evolve into the 2020s. Media history remains relevant for this and other topics, and this researcher hopes that his journalism studies colleagues will utilize this approach in their research, even if it is not their primary method.

References

Primary sources[1]

Trade publications

American Journalism Review
UK *Press Gazette*
Editor & Publisher
Columbia Journalism Review
Society of Professional Journalists' *Quill*

Memoirs/interviews

Addicott, Ruth. Interviews and Correspondence, June 2020.

Ceppos, Jerome Merle ("Jerry)." Interviews and Correspondence, Baton Rouge, Louisiana, May 2020.

Franklin, Bob. Interviews and Correspondence, June 2020.

Fidler, Roger. *Touching the Future: My Odyssey from Print to Online Publishing*. Self-Published, 2019.

Rusbridger, Alan. *Breaking News: The Remaking of Journalism and Why It Matters Now*. New York: Picador, 2017.

Wickham, Kathleen, Interviews and Correspondence, February 2020.

Other primary sources

Knight-Ridder Scenario Planning, 1992/2012, April 1992.

Knight Ridder Management Conference. "Knight Ridder Journalism: Steady Improvement on the Seven Tenets." March 2004.

Shorenstein Center on Media, Politics and Public Policy's "Riptide" Project. www.digitalriptide.org/.

Secondary sources

"About IRE." Investigative Reporters and Editors Inc. Accessed September 8, 2021. www.ire.org/about-ire/.

"About Us: Spot-On Takes Cutting Edge Silicon Valley Technology and Applies It to the Political, Advocacy and Nonprofit Arenas." Accessed September 13, 2021. https://spot-on.com/about.

Allan, Stuart. *Online News: Journalism and the Internet*. Berkshire, UK: Open University Press, 2005.

Alper, Meryl. "Portables, Luggables, and Transportables: Historicizing the Imagined Affordances of Mobile Computing." *Mobile Media & Communication* 7, no. 3 (2019): 322–40.

Ankerson, Megan Sapnar. *Dot-Com Design: The Rise of a Usable, Social, Commercial Web*. New York: New York University Press, 2018.

Anderson, C. W. *Apostles of Certainty: Data journalism and the Politics of Doubt*. New York: Oxford University Press, 2018.

Anonymous Staff Writer. "Edward Lempinen." *Greater Good*. Accessed September 10, 2021. https://greatergood.berkeley.edu/profile/edward_lempinen.

Anonymous Staff Writer. "Microsoft Launches Microsoft Internet Explorer 3.0 with Exclusive, Free Content Offers from Top Web Sites." *Microsoft PressPass*, August 16, 1995. Accessed September 3, 2021. https://news.microsoft.com/1996/08/13/microsoft-launches-microsoft-internet-explorer-3–0-with-exclusive-free-content-offers-from-top-web-sites/.

Anonymous Staff Writer. "BIRTHDAY OF THE DAY: Brian Stelter, Host of CNN's 'Reliable Sources' and Senior Media Correspondent." *Politico*, September 3, 2018. Accessed September 12, 2021. www.politico.com/story/2018/09/03/playbook-birthday-brian-stelter-80629.

Anonymous Staff Writer. "Zuula Unveils Powerful New Internet Search Service." *PRWeb.com*. Accessed September 13, 2021. www.prweb.com/releases/2006/12/prweb490162.htm.

Arrese, Ángel. "From Gratis to Paywalls: A Brief History of a Retro-Innovation in the Press's Business." *Journalism Studies* 17, no. 8 (2016): 1051–67.

Associated Press and RealNetworks. "AP Streaming News with RealNetworks." *Columbia Journalism Review*, March–April 2000, 1.

Atsushi Akera. "Communities and Specialized Information Businesses." In *The Internet and American Business*, edited by William Aspray and Paul Ceruzzi, 423–47. Cambridge, MA: MIT Press, 2008.

Barthel, Michael, Ruth Moon, and Will Mari. "Who Retweets Whom? How Digital and Legacy Journalists Interact on Twitter." *Tow Center for Digital Journalism*, 2015.

Belair-Gagnon, Valerie, and Allison J. Steinke. "Capturing Digital News Innovation Research in Organizations, 1990–2018." *Journalism Studies* 21, no. 12 (2020): 1724–43.

Boczkowski, Pablo. *Digitizing the News: Innovation in Online Newspapers*. Cambridge, MA: MIT Press, 2005.

Bollmer, Grant. *Materialist Media Theory: An Introduction*. New York: Bloomsbury Academic, 2019.

Boyles, Jan Lauren, and Jared Meisinger. "Automation and Adaptation: Reshaping Journalistic Labor in the Newsroom Library." *Convergence: The International Journal of Research into New Media Technologies* 26, no. 1 (2018): 178–92.

Brown, Chip. "State of the American Newspaper. Fear.com." *American Journalism Review* 20, no. 10 (1999): 50–71.

Brügger, Niels. *The Archived Web: Doing History in the Digital Age*. Cambridge, MA: MIT Press, 2018.

Bugeja, Michael. "Computers Keep Reporters in the Office, Off Their Beats." *The Quill*, May 2, 2005. www.quillmag.com/2005/05/02/computers-keep-reporters-in-the-office-off-their-beats/.

Carlson, David. "The History of Online Journalism." In *Digital Journalism: Emerging Media and the Changing Horizons of Journalism*, edited by Kevin Kawamoto, 31–55. Lanham, MD: Rowan & Littlefield, 2003.

Chittum, Ryan. "Audit Interview: Alan D. Mutter." *Columbia Journalism Review*, January 23, 2009. https://archives.cjr.org/the_audit/audit_interview_alan_d_mutter_1.php.

Christensen, Clayton M. *The Innovator's Dilemma: When New Technologies Cause Great Firms to Fail*. Boston, MA: Harvard Business School Press, 1997.

Christensen, Clayton M., Michael E. Raynor, and Rory McDonald. "What Is Disruptive Innovation? Twenty Years After the Introduction of the Theory, We Revisit What It Does—and Doesn't—Explain." *Harvard Business Review*, December 2015. https://hbr.org/2015/12/what-is-disruptive-innovation.

Compaine, Benjamin. "The Online Information Industry." In *Who Owns the Media: Competition and Concentration in the Mass Media Industry*, edited by Benjamin Compaine and Douglas Gomery. Mahwah, NJ: Lawrence Erlbaum Associates, Publishers, 2000.

DeFleur, Margaret. *Computer-Assisted Investigative Reporting: Development and Methodology*. Mahwah, NJ: Lawrence Erlbaum Associates, Publishers, 1997.

DeFleur, Margaret H., and Lucinda D. Davenport. "Innovation Lag: Computer-Assisted Classrooms vs. Newsrooms." *The Journalism Educator* 48, no. 2 (1993): 26–36.

De Maeyer, Juliette. "Content Management Systems and Journalism." *Oxford Research Encyclopedia of Communication*, June 2019.

De Maeyer, Juliette. "Digital Journalism in the Cut-and-paste Era." *Mondes Sociaux*, April 18, 2017. https://sms.hypotheses.org/9407.

Deuze, Mark. "What Is Journalism? Professional Identity and Ideology of Journalists Reconsidered." *Journalism* 6, no. 4 (2015): 442–64.

Deuze, Mark. "Online Journalism: Modeling the First Generation of New Media on the World Wide Web. *First Monday*, November 17, 2003. https://firstmonday.org/article/view/893/802.

Dooley, Patricia L. *The Technology of Journalism: Cultural Agents, Cultural Icons*. Evanston, IL: Northwestern University Press, 2007.

Driscoll, Kevin. "Hobbyist Inter-Networking and the Popular Internet Imaginary: Forgotten Histories of Networked Personal Computing, 1978–1998" (Ph.D. dissertation, University of Southern California, 2015).

Dutton, William H., and Ellen J. Heisper. "The Internet in Britain." *Oxford Internet Survey, Oxford Internet Institute*, 2007. Accessed September 11, 2021. https://oxis.oii.ox.ac.uk/wp-content/uploads/sites/43/2014/11/oxis2007-report.pdf.

Dutton, William H., and Grant Blank. "Next Generation Users: The Internet in Britain." *Oxford Internet Survey, Oxford Internet Institute*, 2011. Accessed September 11, 2021. http://blogs.oii.ox.ac.uk/oxis/wp-content/uploads/sites/43/2014/11/oxis2011-report.pdf.

Earl, Jennifer, and Katrina Kimport. *Digitally Enabled Social Change: Activism in the Internet Age*. Cambridge, MA: MIT Press, 2011.

Emerson, Lori. *Reading Writing Interfaces: From the Digital to the Bookbound*. Minneapolis, MN: University of Minnesota Press, 2014.

Folkenflik, David. "McClatchy Will Buy Knight Ridder for $4.5 Billion." *NPR*, March 13, 2006. www.npr.org/templates/story/story.php?storyId=5260417.

Garrison, Bruce. "Online Newspapers." In *Online News and the Public*, edited by Michael B. Salwen, et al., 3–46. Mahwah, NJ: Lawrence Erlbaum Associations, Publishers, 2005.

Gillmor, Dan. *We the Media: Grassroots Journalism by the People, for the People*. Sebastopol, CA: O'Reilly, 2004.

Griggs, Brandon, and Heather Kelly. "23 Key Moments from Twitter History." *CNN*, September 16, 2013. Accessed September 13, 2021. www.cnn.com/2013/09/13/tech/social-media/twitter-key-moments/index.html.

Godin, Benoit. *Models of Innovation: The History of an Idea*. Cambridge, MA: MIT Press, 2017.

Gunter, Barrie. *News and the Net*. Mahwah, NJ: Lawrence Erlbaum Associations, Publishers, 2003.

Hall, Jim. *Online Journalism: A Critical Primer*. London: Pluto Press, 2001.

Hafner, Katie. *The Well: A Story of Love, Death & Real Life in the Seminal Online Community*. New York: Carroll & Graf Publishers, 2001.

Hao, Karen, and Tanya Basu. "Why Does It Suddenly Feel Like 1999 on the Internet?" *MIT Technology Review*, 2020. www.technologyreview.com/2020/04/03/998480/why-does-it-suddenly-feel-like-1999-on-the-internet/.

Heyward, Anna. "The Story Behind the Unjust Shutdown of Gothamist and DNAinfo." *The New Yorker*, November 14, 2017. Accessed September 12, 2021. www.newyorker.com/culture/culture-desk/the-story-behind-the-unjust-shutdown-of-gothamist-and-dnainfo.

Hicks, Mar. *Programmed Inequality: How Britain Discarded Women Technologists and Lost Its Edge in Computing*. Cambridge, MA: MIT Press, 2017.

Karpf, David. "Something I No Longer Believe: Is Internet Time Slowing Down?" *Social Media + Society*, July–September 2019, 1–4. https://journals.sagepub.com/doi/pdf/10.1177/2056305119849492.

Karpf, David. "25 Years of WIRED Predictions: Why the Future Never Arrives." *WIRED Magazine*, September 18, 2019, 112–20. www.wired.com/story/wired25-david-karpf-issues-tech-predictions/.

King, Elliot. *Free for All: The Internet's Transformation of Journalism*. Evanston, IL: Northwestern University Press, 2010.

Lagorio-Chafkin, Christine. *We Are the Nerds: The Birth and Tumultuous Life of Reddit, the Internet's Culture Laboratory*. New York: Hachette Books, 2018.

LaMorte, Wayne W. "Diffusion of Innovation Theory." Behavioral Change Models, Boston University School of Public Health. Accessed March 10, 2021. https://

sphweb.bumc.bu.edu/otlt/mph-modules/sb/behavioralchangetheories/behavioralchangetheories4.html.

Lehman, Nicolas. "Can Journalism Be Saved? It's Going to Take a Whole New Set of Arrangements, and a New Way of Thinking, to Solve the Present Crisis." *The New York Review of Books*, February 27, 2020. www.nybooks.com/articles/2020/02/27/can-journalism-be-saved/.

Lepore, Jill. "Does Journalism Have a Future? In an Era of Social Media and Fake News, Journalists Who Have Survived the Print Plunge Have New Foes to Face." *The New Yorker*, January 21, 2019. www.newyorker.com/magazine/2019/01/28/does-journalism-have-a-future.

Lingel, Jessa. *An Internet for the People: The Politics and Promise of Craigslist*. Princeton: Princeton University Press, 2020.

Lule, Jack. *Daily News, Eternal Stories: The Mythological Role of Journalism*. New York: The Guilford Press, 2001.

Madden, M., and Lee Rainie. "America's Online Pursuits: The Changing Picture of Who's Online." *Pew Research Center*, 2003. www.pewresearch.org/internet/2003/12/22/americas-online-pursuits/.

Mari, Will. *The American Newsroom: A History, 1920–1960*. Columbia, MO: University of Missouri Press, 2021.

Mari, Will. "A Review Essay: Examining the Fraught Racial, Gendered and Class-Based Origins of the Early Internet and Its Antecedents." *Internet Histories* 4, no. 3 (2020): 349–53.

Mari, Will. "(Electronic) Mailing the Editor: Emails, Message Boards and Early Interactive Web Design in the 1990s." Under Review at the Time of Publication.

Mari, Will. *A Short History of Disruptive Journalism Technologies: 1960–1990*. Abingdon, UK: Routledge, 2019.

Mari, Will. "Technology in the Newsroom: Adoption of the Telephone and the Radio Car from c. 1920 to 1960." *Journalism Studies* 19, no. 9 (2018): 1366–89.

Mari, Will. "Writer by Trade: James Ralph's Claims to Authorship." *Authorship* 4, no. 2 (2015): 1–17.

Mailland, Julien, and Kevin Driscoll. *Minitel: Welcome to the Internet*. Cambridge, MA: MIT Press, 2017.

McCullough, Brian. *How the Internet Happened: From Netscape to the iPhone*. New York: W. W. Norton, 2018.

McKie, David. "Peter Preston Obituary: Guardian Editor Who During 20 Years in the Role Played a Decisive Part in Shaping the Paper's Future." *The Guardian*, January 7, 2018. www.theguardian.com/media/2018/jan/07/peter-preston-obituary.

McIlwain, Charlton. *Black Software: The Internet and Racial Justice, from the Afronet to Black Lives Matter*. Oxford: Oxford University Press, 2019.

Merritt, Davis. *Knight Ridder and How the Erosion of Newspaper Journalism Is Putting Democracy at Risk*. New York: American Management Association, 2005.

Meyer, Philip. *Precision Journalism: A Reporter's Introduction to Social Science Methods*. Bloomington, IN: Indiana University Press.

Meyer, Philip. *The Vanishing Newspaper: Saving Journalism in the Information Age*. 2nd ed. Columbia, MO: University of Missouri, 2009.

Milligan, Ian. *History in the Age of Abundance? How the Web Is Transforming Historical Research*. Montreal, Canada: McGill-Queen's University Press, 2019.

Mitchell, Bill. "How 9/11 Changed Poynter (and Journalism)." *Poynter.org*, September 9, 2021. Accessed September 9, 2021. www.poynter.org/reporting-editing/2021/how-9-11-changed-poynter-and-journalism/.

Moon, Ruth. "Moto-Taxis, Drivers, Weather, and WhatsApp: Contextualizing New Technology in Rwandan Newsrooms." *Journalism* (published online 2021).

Moon, Ruth. "Getting into Living Rooms: NGO Media Relations Work as Strategic Practice." *Journalism* 19, no. 7 (2018): 1011–26.

Moran, Rachel and Nikki Usher. "Objects of Journalism, Revised: Rethinking Materiality in Journalism Studies Through Emotion, Culture and 'Unexpected Objects'." *Journalism* 22, no. 5 (2021): 1155–72.

Negroponte, Nicholas. *Being Digital*. New York: Alfred A. Knopf, 1995.

Newman, Lily Hay. "A Trippy Visualization Charts the Internet's Growth Since 1997 In 2003, Barrett Lyon Created a Map of the Internet. In 2021, He Did It Again—and Showed Just How Quickly It's Expanded." *Wired*, February 21, 2021. www.wired.com/story/opte-internet-map-visualization/?mbid=social_twitter&utm_brand=wired&utm_campaign=falcon&utm_medium=social&utm_social-type=owned&utm_source=twitter/.

Newman, Andy. "Gothamist Will Publish Again in Deal with WNYC." *The New York Times*, February 23, 2018. Accessed September 12, 2021. www.nytimes.com/2018/02/23/nyregion/gothamist-dnainfo-deal-wnyc-publish-again.html.

Ogan, Christine, and Randal Beam. "Internet Challenges for Media Businesses." In *The Internet and American Business*, edited by William Aspray and Paul Ceruzzi, 279–314. Cambridge, MA: The MIT Press, 2008.

Örnebring, Henrik. "Technology and Journalism-as-labor: Historical Perspectives." *Journalism* 11, no. 57 (2010): 57–74.

Örnebring, Henrik, and Amy Schmitz Weiss. "Journalism and the Politics of Mobility." *Journalism Studies* (published online, 2001).

Parks, Perry, and Will Mari. "Teaching CAR: The Computer-Assisted Reporting Movement in Journalism Textbooks, c. 1980–2010." Under Review at the Time of Publication.

Papacharissi, Zizi. "Commentary: Remaking Events, Storytelling and the News." In *Remaking the News: Essays on the Future of Journalism Scholarship in the Digital Age*, edited by Pablo Boczkowski and C. W. Anderson, 147–54. Boston: MIT Press, 2017.

Passaris, Constantine. "Internetization: A New Word for Our Global Economy." *The Conversation*, December 5, 2017. https://theconversation.com/internetization-a-new-word-for-our-global-economy-88013.

Pavlik, John V. *Journalism and New Media*. New York: Columbia University Press, 2001.

Pavlik, John V. "New Technology and News Flows: Journalism and Crisis Coverage." In *Digital Journalism: Emerging Media and the Changing Horizons of Journalism*, edited by Kevin Kawamoto, 75–89. Lanham, MD: Rowan & Littlefield, 2003.

Perrin, Andrew, and Maeve Duggan. "Americans' Internet Access: 2000–2015." *Pew Research Center*, June 26, 2015. Accessed September 11, 2021. www.pewresearch.org/internet/2015/06/26/americans-internet-access-2000-2015/.

Philips, Sarah. "A Brief History of Facebook." *The Guardian*, July 15, 2007. www.theguardian.com/technology/2007/jul/25/media.newmedia.

Picard, Robert, and Jeffrey Brody. *The Newspaper Publishing Industry*. Boston: Allyn and Bacon, 1997.

Plotnick, Rachel. "Tethered Women, Mobile Men: Gendered Mobilities of Typewriting." *Mobile Media & Communication* 8, no. 2 (2020): 188–208.

Porter, David. *Internet Culture*. New York: Routledge, 1997.

Preston, Peter. "The Curse of Introversion." In *The Future of Newspapers*, edited by Bob Franklin, 13–21. London: Routledge, 2009.

Press Gazette Staff. "Our New Website: Cleaner, Quicker and Easier to Use." *Press Gazette*, May 21, 2007. www.pressgazette.co.uk/our-new-website-cleaner-quicker-and-easier-to-use/.

Raine, L. "Modest Increase in Internet Use for Campaign 2002: Modest Increase in Internet Use for Campaign 2002." *Pew Research Center*, 2003. www.pewresearch.org/internet/2003/01/05/modest-increase-in-internet-use-for-campaign-2002/.

Rainie, Lee. "How Americans Used the Internet After the Terror Attack." *Pew Internet & American Life Project*, September 15, 2001. Accessed September 12, 2021. https://webarchive.loc.gov/all/20011008224148/www.pewinternet.org/reports/pdfs/pip_terror_report.pdf.

Rankin, Joy Lisi. *A People's History of Computing in the United States*. Cambridge, MA: Harvard University Press, 2018.

Rogers, Everett. *Diffusion of Innovations*. 4th ed. New York: Free Press, 1995.

Rutten, Tim. "Riordan's Fourth Estate Sending Prototype to Press." *The Los Angeles Times*, January 22, 2003. Accessed September 13, 2021. www.latimes.com/archives/la-xpm-2003-jan-22-et-rutten22-story.html.

Schatzberg, Eric. "Where Do Models of Innovation Come from? Benoit Godin, Models of Innovation." *Technology and Culture* 61, no. 1 (2020): 337–40.

Shafer, Jack. "Don't Blame Craigslist for the Decline of Newspapers." *Politico*, December 13, 2016. www.politico.com/magazine/story/2016/12/craigslist-newspapers-decline-classifieds-214525.

Shapiro, Michael. "The Newspaper That Almost Seized the Future." *The Columbia Journalism Review*, November–December 2011. https://archives.cjr.org/feature/the_newspaper_that_almost_seized_the_future.php.

Shapiro, Michael, Anna Hiatt, and Mike Hoy. *Tales from the Great Disruption: Insights and Lessons from Journalism's Technological Transformation*. Minneapolis, MN: Big Roundtable Books, 2015.

Shepard, Alicia. "Craig Newmark and Craigslist Didn't Destroy Newspapers, They Outsmarted Them." *USA Today*, June 17, 2018. www.usatoday.com/story/opinion/2018/06/18/craig-newmark-craigslist-didnt-kill-newspapers-outsmarted-them-column/702590002/.

Singer, Leif. "On the Diffusion of Innovations: How New Ideas Spread." Accessed March 10, 2021. https://leif.me/on-the-diffusion-of-innovations-how-new-ideas-spread/.

Speer, John C. "The New Century Network: A Critical Moment for Newspapers at the Dawn of the Internet" (MA thesis, University of Maryland, 2013).

Staff Report. "Household Internet Use Survey." *The Daily*, Statistics Canada, July 26, 2001. Accessed September 11, 2001. https://www150.statcan.gc.ca/n1/daily-quotidien/010726/dq010726a-eng.htm; Staff Report. "Canadian Internet Use Survey." Statistics Canada, January 1, 2013. Accessed September 11, 2021. https://www150.statcan.gc.ca/n1/daily-quotidien/110525/dq110525b-eng.htm.

Staff Report. "The State of the News Media 2006." *Pew*, March 13, 2006. Accessed September 13, 2021. www.pewtrusts.org/en/research-and-analysis/reports/2006/03/13/the-state-of-the-news-media-2006.

Stelter, Brian. "MSNBC.com May Change Its Name." *The New York Times*, October 6, 2010. Accessed September 3, 2021. www.nytimes.com/2010/10/07/business/media/07msnbc.html.

Stovall, James Glen. *Web Journalism: Practice and Promise of a New Medium*. Boston: Pearson, 2004.

Streeter, Thomas. *The Net Effect: Romanticism, Capitalism and the Internet*. New York: NYU Press, 2010.

Streitfeld, David. "Craig Newmark, Newspaper Villain, Is Working to Save Journalism." *New York Times*, October 17, 2018. www.nytimes.com/2018/10/17/technology/craig-newmark-journalism-gifts.html.

Thompson, Estes. "McClatchy to buy The News & Observer of Raleigh." *Associated Press*, May 17, 1995. https://apnews.com/article/4bb031aea8b9d427b34f37dfeeff4ae2.

Tunstall, Jeremy. *The Media Were American: U.S. Mass Media in Decline*. 2nd ed. New York: Oxford University Press, 2007.

Turvill, William. "Piers Morgan 'Resigns' and Six-Strong Team Launches Website for Daily Mail: Ten Years Ago This Week." *Press Gazette*, May 14, 2014. www.pressgazette.co.uk/piers-morgan-resigns-and-six-strong-team-launches-website-for-daily-mail-ten-years-ago-this-week/.

Usher, Nikki. "Newsroom Moves and the Newspaper Crisis Evaluated: Space, Place, and Cultural Meaning." *Media, Culture & Society* 37, no. 7 (2015): 1005–21.

U.S. Census Bureau. "Statistical Abstract of the United States: 1996, Section 1. Population." October 1996, 1. www.census.gov/library/publications/1996/compendia/statab/116ed.html.

Walker, Mason. "U.S. Newsroom Employment Has Fallen 26% Since 2008." *Pew Research Center*, July 13, 2021. Accessed September 14, 2021. www.pewresearch.org/fact-tank/2021/07/13/u-s-newsroom-employment-has-fallen-26-since-2008/.

Weiss, Amy Schmitz, and David Domingo. "Innovation Processes in Online Newsrooms as Actor-Networks and Communities of Practice." *New Media & Society* 12, no. 7 (2010): 1156–71.

Wendland, Mike. "Overloaded Internet Fails Info-starved Americans." *Detroit Free Press*, September 11, 2001. Accessed September 12, 2001. http://web.archive.org/web/20020611064222/www.poynter.org/Terrorism/Mike1.htm.

Wickham, Kathleen, ed. *Perspectives: Online Journalism*. Boulder: CourseWise Pub, 1998.

Williams, Paul. *The Computerized Newspaper: A Practical Guide for Systems Users*. Oxford: Heinemann Professional Publishing Ltd., 1990.

Whitehead, Beth, Deborah Andrews, Amip Shah, and Graeme Maidment. "Assessing the Environmental Impact of Data Centres Part 1: Background, Energy Use and Metrics." *Building and Environment* 82 (August 2014): 151–59.

Zuckerman, Ethan. "The Internet's Original Sin It's Not Too Late to Ditch the Ad-based Business Model and Build a Better Web." *The Atlantic*, August 14, 2014. www.theatlantic.com/technology/archive/2014/08/advertising-is-the-internets-original-sin/376041/.

Note

1 For more on the use of primary sources, see the notes on methods and sources in the introduction.

Index

For Product Safety Concerns and Information please contact our EU representative GPSR@taylorandfrancis.com Taylor & Francis Verlag GmbH, Kaufingerstraße 24, 80331 München, Germany

Printed and bound by CPI Group (UK) Ltd, Croydon, CR0 4YY
15/09/2026
02217072-0001